LY11/23　　　　Play

Gallery Books
Editor: Peter Fallon

CYRANO DE BERGERAC

Derek Mahon

CYRANO DE BERGERAC

A new version of
Edmond Rostand's 'heroic comedy'

Gallery Books

Cyrano de Bergerac
is first published
simultaneously in paperback
and in a clothbound edition
on the day of its première,
19 April 2004.

The Gallery Press
Loughcrew
Oldcastle
County Meath
Ireland

ISBN 1 85235 358 9 (*paperback*)
     1 85235 359 7 (*clothbound*)

A CIP catalogue record for this book
is available from the British Library.

The Gallery Press acknowledges the financial assistance of An Chomhairle Ealaíon / The Arts Council, Ireland.

for Stephen Rea

This version of *Cyrano de Bergerac* was first produced by the National Theatre, London, on 19 April 2004, with the following cast:

CYRANO	Stephen Rea
ROXANE	Claire Price
CHRISTIAN	Zubin Varla
RAGUENEAU	Anthony O'Donnell
DE GUICHE	Malcolm Storry
DEBRAY	Nick Sampson
GENEVIÈVE	Katherine Manners
LIGNIÈRE	Mark Bonnar
VALVERT	Pascal Langdale
MONTFLEURY	Stephen Critchlow
JODELET	David Collings
LIZ	Mairéad McKinley
CASTEL-JALOUX	Gregory Fox-Murphy
MARIANNE	Katy Odey
CADETS	
BILL	Simon Merrells
JULES	Mark Bonnar
PATRICK	Thomas Arnold
BRIAN	Dermot Kerrigan
HUGH	Harry Peacock
GUS	Pascal Langdale
JACQUES	William Rycroft
NUNS	
MARGUERITE	Mairéad McKinley
ANNE	Katy Odey
CLAIRE	Katherine Manners
BERTRAND	Daniel Tuite
SENTRY	Trevor Thomas
PIERRE/DANCER	Stephen Berkeley-White
MARTIN/DANCER	Gildas Diquero
GARANCE/DANCER	Joanne Fong
AURÉLIA/DANCER	Antonia Grove
ILLUMINEUSE/DANCER	Miranda Lind
JEAN/DANCER	Tam Ward

MUSICIANS
   Bruce O'Neil (MD/accordion)
   Katherine Toy (accordion)
   Toby Kelly (saxophone)
   Corrina Silvester (percussion)
   Jeremy Wiles (percussion)

Other parts played by members of the company.

Director	Howard Davies
Set Designer	William Dudley
Costume Designer	John Bright
Lighting Designer	Paul Anderson
Music	Dominic Muldowney
Movement and Dance	Christopher Bruce
Fight Director	William Hobbs
Sound Designer	Paul Groothuis
Literal Translation	Christopher Campbell

Foreword

Cyrano de Bergerac opened in Paris in 1897 and has remained in the international repertoire ever since. There are now, in English, highly actable versions by Christopher Fry, Anthony Burgess and others, and it's always on somewhere in some form; for, not only is it a play, it has been film and musical too. Several films, in fact, most recently Jean-Paul Rappeneau's terrific 1990 release with Depardieu in the title role and English subtitles by Burgess. The old rascal is popular too in China and Japan since he is, after all, an adept of *bushido* and the martial arts; and, aside from his nose, what distinguishes Cyrano (the stress falls on the first syllable) is the confrontational aplomb he calls his 'panache' — literally, the decorative plume in his hat. Rostand proposed panache as a philosophy of life: something fanciful and performative, 'the kind of courage which, at ease in situations, frames and defines them with wit. If renunciation or sacrifice are involved, it's a consolation of attitude one adopts.'

The play is itself distinguished by panache in its remarkable lyrical fluency and in the defiant myth it sets up as an alternative to the cynical materialism we now take for granted; also in its cult of illusion and the defining moment — what Yeats called 'character isolated by a deed' (Cyrano dies like Cúchulainn). Described in its time as a 'fake masterpiece', and more charitably by George Steiner as 'gorgeous nonsense', the play gave rise in some quarters to the hope of a new verse drama. But no, it was *sui generis*, a flash in the pan — though echoes of Rostand's dream music lingered in the work of Alain-Fournier, Proust and Cocteau, whose mythic films owe much to Rostand's scenic elegance; traditional legend and fairy story nourished both. *Cyrano* is Rostand's 'Beauty and the Beast', its protagonist a creature of fairy tale who speaks directly to childhood memory, even to the unconscious. Roxane is a student of Mother Goose; and when her coach, 'like the pumpkin in the fairy tale', appears among the besieged Cadets, she is Snow White, girl and mother, among the Dwarves: 'Good fairy!' says Cyrano. Balcony scene and convent garden have the ambrosial, moonlit, metamorphic atmosphere of *A Midsummer Night's Dream*.

The present version, a 19th-century play set in the 17th century and intended for 21st-century production, embraces with enthusiasm what Borges called 'the vulgar pleasures of anachronism'. We are in indeterminate space-time — the France of 1640 (Louis XIII on the throne), though the war looks remarkably like that of 1914-1918. The Gascons are a sort of Ulstermen, the *précieuses* modern feminists; the theatrical milieu owes something to 18th-century Drury Lane and 20th-century Broadway. The musicians sing a mediaeval pop song, but Hubble has already proposed (as he did in 1929) the now familiar notion of an expanding universe. The historical Cyrano (1619-1656), himself a serious astronomer, might not have been too surprised.

Derek Mahon

CYRANO DE BERGERAC

ACT ONE

Dark theatre; June evening, dusk. An empty house, dim light. Enter, from different doors, DOORMAN *and two* OFFICERS.

DOORMAN

So, where's your ticket?

1ST OFFICER
                    Are you speaking to me?
I'm a captain in the Royal Household Cavalry.

DOORMAN

And you?

2ND OFFICER
            Lieutenant, Rifle Corps.

1ST OFFICER
                    I see
we're early for the play — an empty hall —
so let's get in some practice with the foil.

They practise, feint and fence. Enter various BLOKES *and* GIRLS.

1st BLOKE
(*to* BLOKES; *he shuffles and deals*)
A quick flutter? The candle and Bordeaux
come grace of my employer, don't you know.

2ND BLOKE
(*to* GIRL)
Give us a kiss before they light the light.

GIRL
People can see.

2ND BLOKE
Down here we're out of sight.

1ST BLOKE
The knave of clubs . . .

3RD BLOKE
. . . I trump you with a heart.

Enter various SPECTATORS *including* THIEVES.

1ST SPECTATOR
(*producing a snack*)
If you want a quick bite this is the perfect place.

2ND SPECTATOR
(*opening a bottle*)
And a drinking man can drink his wine in peace.

Enter BOURGEOIS *and* SON.

BOURGEOIS
You'd think we'd strayed into some frightful slum.
Drinkers, robbers, ruffians . . . God's grace,
and they first played *Le Cid* in this very room!

Enter BOYS; *one boyish* GIRL.

DOORMAN
You lot behave yourselves!

1ST BOY
(*with wounded dignity*)
What, us do you mean?
. . . Have we the fish hooks and the fishing line?
Got a pea-shooter?

2ND BOY
Yes, and we got peas.

Enter MARIANNE *with drinks tray; audience slowly gathers.*

1ST BOY
. . . The girl I told you about? Look, there she is.
Hey, Marianne, you speaking to us tonight?

MARIANNE *ignores them.*

BOURGEOIS
Gamblers and fornicators, if you please.
It's shameful to see people of this sort
disporting themselves in a temple of high art.

STAGEHANDS *prepare chandeliers for lighting and hoisting.*

1ST SPECTATOR
Can't see a fucking thing; let there be light!

THIEF
(*to* THIEVES)
Okay, you novices to the cut-purse racket,
I'm going to show you how to pick a pocket.
Change is noisy; careful you don't shake it.

2ND SPECTATOR
Who's on tonight?

BOURGEOIS
It's Montfleury who plays.

17

Milk, lemonade, pippins, cinnamon, nuts, canapés.

Enter two MARQUISES; *also* MUSICIANS *and* JODELET *the theatre manager.*

1ST MARQUIS
We arrive like tradesmen in an empty vault
with no one here to sneer at and insult?
Who are these trash? Let's find our usual chairs.

One MARQUIS *eyes the* BOYS; *sniffs cocaine from snuff box.*

1ST SPECTATOR
Strike up the music! Hoist the chandeliers!

A STAGEHAND *lights and hoists chandeliers; the* MUSICIANS —
lute, tabor, oboe, fiddle, flute — strike up a pop song:

I saw her standing there
Beside the *porte-cochère.*
All are in love with her:
Which one will she prefer?
Good fortune would it be
Did she decide on me,
Did she decide on me.

Enter ACADEMICIANS; *also* LIGNIÈRE *and* CHRISTIAN; LIGNIÈRE
a distinguished drunk, CHRISTIAN *a handsome but provincial young man.*

1ST MARQUIS
Lignière, not drunk yet?

LIGNIÈRE
(*to* CHRISTIAN)
Shall I introduce you?
. . . Gentlemen, Baron Christian de Neuchâteau,
here from Touraine just a few days ago.

CHRISTIAN

I've hardly been in Paris a week yet;
I start tomorrow as a Guards cadet.
I feel as if I'm still on the high-road.

2ND MARQUIS
(*aside*)
A handsome chap, though scarcely *à la mode*.

SON
(*to* BOURGEOIS)
Papa, are those the *Académie française*?

BOURGEOIS
. . . Boudou; Boudeau . . . All the immortals, yes.

THIEF
(*to* THIEVES)
You lift a fob-watch with a handkerchief.

BOYS *shoot peas and fish for wigs.*

1ST ACADEMICIAN
My best peruque! Boy, do you dare to laugh?
Have you no respect for your elders?

1ST BOY
                                    Get a life!

2ND ACADEMICIAN
My new hair-piece! How dare you? I shan't fail
to report you to the management.

2ND BOY
                                    Keep it real!

Enter PRÉCIEUSES.

1ST MARQUIS

Here come the ladies, each one a *précieuse* —
Aurélia, Geneviève, Garance, Illumineuse.

CHRISTIAN

What are *précieuses*? Great beauties, do you mean?

LIGNIÈRE

Bluestocking wits, the smartest girls in town.

CHRISTIAN

What gorgeous names. Are you acquainted with them?

2ND MARQUIS

Acquainted? I've known most of them in my time.

LIGNIÈRE

I'm here at your request but I don't think
the lady's coming, and I need a drink.

CHRISTIAN

Don't leave me; you're the only person here
can help me with this woman that I admire.
I'm afraid she'll be too clever and refined.
I get tongue-tied; I haven't a quick mind.
It scares me stiff, the way they think and write:
their flowery talk, so chic and . . . erudite.
I'm just a soldier, not a brilliant wit.
. . . One box still empty, up there on the right.

MARIANNE

Milk, lemonade, mineral water?

LIGNIÈRE

                    Thank you, no;
I'd put paid to a pint of claret, though.
Here comes the baker poet Ragueneau.

Enter RAGUENEAU, *an amiable, slightly comical figure.*

RAGUENEAU

Good evening, gentlemen. No sign of Cyrano?

LIGNIÈRE

Ragueneau hosts an aspiring poetry group
twice weekly in the back of his coffee shop.
His fellow poets get free cakes and tarts;
himself a poet, while he bakes he writes.

RAGUENEAU

You do me too much honour, monsieur Lignière.

LIGNIÈRE

Be quiet, poet, Mycaenas that you are.
Do you like the theatre too?

RAGUENEAU

Of course I do.
No sign of Cyrano? How strange.

LIGNIÈRE

Why so?

RAGUENEAU

Why so? The 'great' Montfleury's on tonight.

LIGNIÈRE

What's that to Cyrano?

RAGUENEAU

But don't you know?
Montfleury, whom he hates, he's told to desist
from any performance for a month at least.

LIGNIÈRE

Montfleury's advertised; he can't stop the show.

RAGUENEAU

We shall soon see.

1ST MARQUIS
Who is this Cyrano?

JODELET
A sort of swordsman poet, a rapier wit.

2ND MARQUIS
A nobleman?

JODELET
As noble as you can get —
a Gascon squire, and we all know what *they're* like.
His friend Debray can put you on the right track.

> *Enter* DEBRAY, *an anxious and serious man; he searches among
> the crowd before joining the* LIGNIÈRE *group.*

DEBRAY
I'm looking for my old friend de Bergerac.

1ST MARQUIS
A most remarkable figure, I've been told.

DEBRAY
The most remarkable in the entire world —
soldier, poet, physicist; so versatile.

LIGNIÈRE
Extraordinary full-face, even more so in profile.

RAGUENEAU
Cyrano's no oil painting, to be sure.
Absurd, flamboyant, singular, bizarre,
his slouch hat feathered like an outward sign
of the extravagant spirit lodged within,
his old cape flung theatrically back
so the rapier sticks out like a fighting cock;
and what a profile, what a glorious snout!
When you set eyes on it you want to shout:

'Heavens, that schnozzle really takes the cake!'
As proud as Punch he steps out with his great dong.
You think he'll take it off, it's a false face —
but no, the bloody thing remains in place;
and that's our friend de Bergerac.

DEBRAY

A tongue
that would clip tin; a fierce man with a sword:
woe betide anyone who says a word.

Enter ROXANE, *to admiring glances, and takes her seat.*

1ST MARQUIS

God, what a beautiful woman; look up there.
Heavens, her figure; and her eyes, her hair:
a glowing peach with the dew still upon her.

2ND MARQUIS

Oh yes, but so protective of her honour,
so hoity-toity, so serene, so cool;
if you went near her you would catch a chill.

CHRISTIAN
(*to* LIGNIÈRE)

... That's her!

LIGNIÈRE

Oh yes?

CHRISTIAN
Quick, tell me who she is.

LIGNIÈRE

Why, that's Roxane, one of our young *précieuses* —
bookish, artistic, feminist don't you know;
an orphan, single, some cousin of Cyrano ...

Enter DE GUICHE, *elegant and proud; with* VALVERT, *foppish and conceited.*

... the Count de Guiche, who dotes on her, although
nephew-in-law of the great Richelieu
and a keen advocate of the coming war.
He aims to marry her off to that Valvert,
complaisant, dim, who wouldn't turn a hair.
She hates it, being a woman of more sense;
but this de Guiche, with power and influence,
could make life very difficult, if he chose,
for an innocent, inexperienced bourgeoise.
I've just exposed the whole sinister plot
in the social column I write for the *Gazette*.

CHRISTIAN

I'm going to have a word with this Valvert.

LIGNIÈRE

Oh no. Besides, she's noticed you; look there.
I'm the one who's leaving; stay where you are.
I've things to attend to in the Zig-Zag Bar.

Exit unsteadily.

DEBRAY

No Cyrano.

RAGUENEAU

I must say I'm surprised.

DEBRAY

Maybe he didn't see Montfleury advertised ...

Indicates DE GUICHE. *Thieves approach* CHRISTIAN *who is gazing at* ROXANE.

... Another Gascon, but the worldly sort,
cunning and cold, the kind that thrives at court.

DE GUICHE

Good evening, gentlemen; is this my chair?
When does the play begin? Sit here, Valvert.

CHRISTIAN

So that's my rival?
                    (*notices* THIEF)
              ... What are you doing there,
picking my pocket?

THIEF

                    If you release me, sir,
I'll let you in on a secret. Your friend Lignière,
the writing gentleman, is as good as dead;
something he wrote has angered a great lord.
A hundred men are at the Porte de Nesle
to catch him weaving home and crack his skull.

CHRISTIAN

I've got to warn him; where would I find him now?

THIEF

Go round the public houses; try the Plough,
the Café Rouge, the Rosebud, the Zig-Zag Bar,
and leave a note at each if he's not there.

CHRISTIAN

Okay. The cowards: a hundred against one!
I hate to leave here but I must be gone;
the important thing right now is to save Lignière.

Exit CHRISTIAN; *enter, obscurely,* RICHELIEU.

1ST SPECTATOR

When does this tedious pastoral crap begin?

2ND SPECTATOR

Richelieu, look, in the curtained box up there.

1ST SPECTATOR
Richelieu is here, so what's the big delay?

2ND SPECTATOR
Why are we waiting? Start the bloody play!

ALL
Montfleury, Montfleury; hurray, hurray!

> *The curtain opens; a pastoral scene. Enter* MONTFLEURY, *a huge
> fat man got up incongruously as a shepherd, a flowery cap over
> one ear, beribboned bagpipes in hand, who bows in acknowledge-
> ment and strikes an ingratiating attitude.*

MONTFLEURY
(*declaims*)
Happy the man who, far from civic rage,
lives all alone in his own golden age
where breezes whisper through the woodland air . . .

> *A brisk, sarcastic voice interrupts from the auditorium.*

CYRANO
(*off*)
I warned you, imbecile; did you not hear?
Gargantuan idiot, kindly leave the stage!

MONTFLEURY
(*uncertainly*)
Happy the man who, far from civic rage . . .

CYRANO
(*off*)
Do you still persist in this dull verbiage?
Do you want my stick to whisper round your ear?

MONTFLEURY
(*nervously*)
Happy the man . . .

26

CYRANO
(*off*)
Get out!

MONTFLEURY
(*wretchedly*)
. . . Happy the man . . .

CYRANO
(*off*)
I've warned you and I won't warn you again!

3RD SPECTATOR
Ignore him, Montfleury; the man's a pain.

Drawn by curiosity, commedia dell'arte figures appear from backstage; contending voices.

4TH SPECTATOR
Go on, Montfleury; you with the beak, shut up.
We paid to see the play, so zip the lip.

Whistles, farmyard noises; cock-a-doodle-doo; riotous interventions.

5TH SPECTATOR
If that low crowd from the rue St Denis
sat down, perhaps the rest of us could see.

6TH SPECTATOR
If those hired killers from the rue de Seine
shut up, perhaps we'll hear what's going on.

5TH SPECTATOR
Your father, whom you first met late in life,
sired two fat children on his brother's wife.

6TH SPECTATOR
Your sister, under cover of prostitution,
provides the watch with helpful information.

5TH SPECTATOR
I'll get you afterwards, you piece of shit!

MONTFLEURY
(*to* MARQUISES)
Gentlemen, help me!

1ST MARQUIS
Oh, get on with it!

CYRANO *bounds on stage from the auditorium waving a stick.*

CYRANO
The gentry to remain, please, in their places
before my stick tickles their dainty arses.
If this impostor doesn't leave at once
I won't be answerable for the consequence.
Okay, you've asked for it, since you refuse.

MONTFLEURY
(*indignantly*)
Insulting me, you insult the Tragic Muse.

CYRANO
(*politely*)
Should the Muse, sir, for whom you don't exist,
have the misfortune to be introduced
to your fat face and your extraneous weight,
she'd kick your backside with her thigh-length boot.
. . . If this continues, think of my poor sword;
it loves to leap out of its own accord.

4TH SPECTATOR
You bugger off, monsieur de Bric-à-Brac;
we want the play, or else our money back!

BLOKE
(*sings*)
We've had enough
Of Cyrano;
So call his bluff.
On with the show!

4TH SPECTATOR
Enough of Cyranose, on with the show!

CROWD
... the show! On with the show! On with the show!

CYRANO
If I hear, just once more, these idiot lines
I'll bring the roof down on you philistines.

4TH SPECTATOR
So, Cyrano, now you're Samson, is that it?

CYRANO
Lend me your jaw-bone and you'll soon find out.

AURÉLIA
Disgraceful!

GARANCE
Scandalous!

BOURGEOIS
A shocking sight:
what a bear-garden!

1ST BOY
Glad you came?

2ND BOY
You bet!

CYRANO

Be quiet and listen to me. I now invite
you heroes in the audience here tonight
to solitary combat, blade to blade.
Let's have some names; come on, don't be afraid.
One at a time; who wants to be the first?
Whoever wants a go, stick up your fist.
You, sir? No. You? Or you? Sir, will you try?
Hands up those valiant ones who wish to die.
. . . My naked blade's too much for your pudeur?
No names? No hands? Right, as I've said before,
I want the theatre cured of this gumboil:
if not, I lance it with my personal foil.
I'll clap three times, you goitre, you absurd
moon-face; eclipse yourself before the third.

He claps slowly twice.

MONTFLEURY

On further reflection, everything considered . . .

Exit.

JODELET

The distinguished actor you so much admire
has been obliged to suddenly retire . . .

4TH SPECTATOR

Montfleury, take no notice; get back here!

1ST SPECTATOR

Go live alone in your own woodland air!

CROWD

Good riddance to bad rubbish! Coward! Boo-boo!

Whistling, slow clapping; audience starts to disperse.

GIRL

Why do you hate Montfleury as you do?

CYRANO

I have two reasons, my young *ingénue*,
each of them quite sufficient on its own —
first, he's the sort who puffs out ponderously
dramatic verse which should be made to fly;
my other reason is a private one . . .
(*to* PRÉCIEUSES)
. . . I'm sorry to disappoint you gorgeous dames,
poets yourselves, the poetry in our dreams.

JODELET

The box-office receipts, monsieur de Bergerac —
what of the cash I have to give them back?

CYRANO

You're right, of course; the theatre can't go bust.
Will a few quid make up for what you've lost?

JODELET

Thank you; and may I say, on terms like these,
you can shut the theatre any night you please.

Dispersing audience pauses as the following scene unfolds.

NUISANCE
(*to* CYRANO)

I think it scandalous you should disparage
the finest actor on the modern stage,
a man with a patron of great influence.
Who patronizes you, Sir Cinzano?

CYRANO

Who patronizes me? No powerful prince.

NUISANCE

You'd better leave.

31

CYRANO

No, you're the one to go;
but, out of interest, just before you do,
explain to me why you're staring at my nose.
An odd shape, do you think? Swarming with flies?
Somewhat disfigured? An unusual size?
You flat-faced lowbrow, don't you realize
I'm vastly proud of the fine orifice
I sport here in the place between my eyes,
though I look to you like a creature from outer space.

NUISANCE

(*nervously*)

It's quite cute really.

CYRANO

Cute, did you say cute?
Are you blind, man? Mine is a *glorious* snout.
A nose like this distinguished the belovèd
poet of the *Amores*, immortal Ovid;
nor do we grant ourselves a foolish giggle
at the author of *Dead Souls*, the mighty Gogol.
Such a proboscis is the certain sign
of a brave and generous nature, truly fine,
such as my own; while your inglorious face,
moron, evinces not the slightest trace
of pride, imagination, poetry, tact,
sparkle or character, of *nose* in fact,
deserving only of the use of force,
a smack in the gob or a fast toe up the arse.

NUISANCE

Call out the watch!

Exit.

CYRANO

(*to his audience*)
A word to the unwise

who mock my blower with an insolent gaze.

DE GUICHE
His exhibitionism is growing tedious.

VALVERT
Wait here, I'll put the hooligan in his place.
                    (*to* CYRANO, *showing off to* ROXANE)
Your blower, sir, is too big for your face.

CYRANO
That's it? Is that the best you can think of?
Let's try to find some livelier alternative
by varying the tone . . . for example, how about:
Critical: 'Sir, if I'd a nose like that
I'd cut it off without a second thought.'
Convivial: 'Does it not get in your wine?
I'd favour a hip-flask if it was mine.'
Health-conscious: 'Sir, when you light up your briar,
does it not set the whole neighbourhood on fire?'
Sociable: 'Watch out, chatting up the chicks,
you don't tip forward down their open necks.'
Pedantic: 'What a terrific signifier;
only the elephant in Aristophanes
can have had so much trunk with which to sneeze!'
Touristy: 'Sir, excuse us if we stare:
it's more than a Cap Gris Nez, it's a Finistère!
Would you mind very much if we took a photograph?'
Jokey: 'Enter it in a contest for a laugh;
it's sure to walk off with the biggest prize.'
Rustic: 'Oi niver seen a spud that soize.'
Dramatic, murmuring through parted lips:
'Is this the nose that sank a thousand ships?'
Burlesque: 'Hey, buddy, don't believe a woird:
take it from Schnozzle, de whole woirld's absoird!'
There, more or less, is what you might have said
if you'd any wit or loirning in your head.

DE GUICHE
Valvert, you'd better leave it.

VALVERT
(*furious*)
What a slob,
a cheap provincial dressed like a mad yob.

CYRANO
Mine is a moral elegance of the mind.
Smarter than fops like you, if less refined,
I face the world with an unclouded stare,
my honour glittering and my conscience clear.
My independence shines out with panache,
my spirit bristles like a stiff moustache;
covered with glory, bright with reputation,
I have no need to be a slave of fashion;
soul-slim, and acting out my life with flair,
I strike for my own truth like a sparkling spur.

VALVERT
(*spitting with rage*)
A bumptious clown; a certifiable maniac.

CYRANO
How do you do? I'm Cyrano de Bergerac.

VALVERT
. . . A poet . . .

CYRANO
Yes, a poet; and, for your insolence,
I'll improvise some verses while we fence
and drive the point home with my final line.

   Both draw swords, audience tense with anticipation, while
   CYRANO *suits his actions to his words.*

Will the light sabre suit you? Shall we dance?

34

Give me a minute to pick my rhymes . . . Begin.

> I cast aside my feathery hat
> And gracefully remove my cloak
> Revealing my athletic cut,
> The rippling muscles of my back;
> Magnificent from toe to tit,
> Sensational as an ancient Greek,
> I warn you, ineffectual twit,
> That on the final line I strike.
>
> I foil your timorous thrust, my dear,
> And you back off as pale as puke.
> There's a fly buzzing at your ear
> But I dispatch it with a flick;
> Also your buttons and bows, I fear,
> Of which I've never seen the like.
> You'll rue your insolence, d'you hear,
> When, at the final line, I strike.
>
> Better if you had shut your trap
> And not provoked a ticklish bloke.
> Where shall I nick you, impotent pup,
> The heart, the vitals or the neck?
> I see you're trying to find a gap
> But you're no match for my technique.
> The joke is over, the game is up
> As, with the final line . . . I strike!

VALVERT *falls; brouhaha; contending voices.*

OFFICER

Spectacular!

AURÉLIA

So stylish!

DEBRAY

Quite insane!

SPECTATORS
. . . Congratulations . . . my compliments . . . well done.
What nerve, verve . . . what elegance; what aplomb!

1ST MARQUIS
Disgraceful; who is this violent parvenu?

6TH SPECTATOR
You'd better fuck off or we'll get you too!

1ST MARQUIS
What, an illiterate guttersnipe like you?

6TH SPECTATOR
Montaigne says those who use talcum powder
do so to disguise some painful natural odour.

1ST MARQUIS
By God I'll split him from the groin to the gums!

6TH SPECTATOR
Come on, then, you and your shirt-lifting chums!

JODELET
Gentlemen, please; there are ladies in the theatre!

6TH SPECTATOR
We'll do the men first and the women later!

1ST OFFICER
(*to* CYRANO)
I've some experience in these matters too
and I congratulate you. What a show!

JODELET
(*to theatre staff*)
. . . Clean up, close up, but don't put out the light;
we're coming back here when we've had a bite
to read through the new comedy for Monday.

Poor Montfleury: *sic transit gloria mundi.*

Crowd disperses.

DEBRAY

Cyrano, aren't you dining with us?

CYRANO

No,
I'm out of pocket: all my monthly dough.

DEBRAY

What will you live on, what will you use for cash?
What lunacy.

CYRANO

Ah yes, but what panache.

MARIANNE

I hate to see you undernourished, sir;
please help yourself to anything you see here.

CYRANO

Dear girl, though it would wound my Gascon pride
to rob you of your delicious stock-in-trade,
I daren't refuse you; chivalry demands
I take a nibble from your gentle hands —
a grape, some mineral water, a slice of bread.

He accepts nourishment.

DEBRAY

This is the stupidest thing I ever heard.

MARIANNE

Take something more, sir.

CYRANO

No, only your hand.

37

(*kisses her hand; to* DEBRAY)
. . . God, I was starving. Now, what's on your mind?

DEBRAY

These vicious ninnies of the ignorant kind
will drive you mad with their impertinence
if they can interfere with your good sense;
but what reaction will this entertainment
arouse among the people who really count?

CYRANO

A vigorous one.

DEBRAY

Exactly; don't you know
Richelieu himself was there in his usual place?

CYRANO

Really? I do hope he enjoyed the show.
An author in his own right, he must have smiled
to see the competition so reviled.

DEBRAY

You're cutting off your nose to spite your face;
you've made too many enemies with this farce.

CYRANO

How many, would you say, at a rough guess?

DEBRAY

De Guiche, Valvert, that Montfleury of course,
those present of the *Académie française*.

CYRANO

Splendid.

DEBRAY

But what's the system, why do you do this?

CYRANO

I was lost in a wood for years, vague and bemused.
Everything seemed so difficult, so confused,
so many choices I was spoilt for choice;
but I found the simplest path out to the light,
the obvious way to live in the world again:
working at everything with flair and grace
to shine at all things and to live for that.

DEBRAY

Okay; but, truthfully now, can you explain
why this Montfleury gives you such a pain?

CYRANO

The pompous windbag has a waist so thick
I doubt if he could reach to his own dick
yet thinks himself a great hit with the women.
I can't abide the posturing, the common
audience-ogling of the bloated toad,
especially since the night he even dared
let his gaze rest on someone in particular,
vilely besmirching with his slimy glance
a certain young lady of my acquaintance
like a snail crawling over an innocent flower.

DEBRAY

And who is the young lady, may I inquire?

CYRANO

The young lady? I whose ridiculous nose
precedes me like a lamp wherever it goes,
excluded from a love of genuine worth,
I love, of course, the loveliest girl on earth,
the finest, best — a star danced at her birth —
but a grave danger unconscious of her effect,
exquisite although ignorant of the fact,
a natural magnet, a rose-scented trap
where love lies waiting for some fortunate chap.
He knows perfection who has known her smile,

her quiet distinction, beauty without guile,
her serious grace and unpretentious style.
Not Aphrodite on her shingled shore
nor virgin Artemis in her forest bower
gave off such light in ages dead and gone
as when she moves through Paris.

DEBRAY
                    My God: Roxane.

CYRANO
Of course: Roxane.

DEBRAY
                    So speak to her: why not?
She gazed at you with devotion here tonight.

CYRANO
Now look, and tell me honestly, what hope
can I have with this preposterous telescope?
I've no illusions; yet I pause sometimes
in a dark evening park where ivy climbs
and sniff the blue scent of a summer night.
I follow with my gaze in the moonlight
some fellow with a girlfriend on his arm,
wishing I too might be at peace like them.
I'm happy; I forget; then, like a fool,
I see my shadow on the garden wall!

    Sniffs audibly.

You know, sometimes it makes me miserable,
this hideous knob; but I refuse to snivel —
there's nothing uglier than a tear that flows
down the grim length of a ridiculous nose;
I won't devalue, for my own relief,
the sacred mystery of celestial grief.

    Commedia dell'arte figures regroup and rehearse backstage.

DEBRAY

Don't be so sad; love works by chance alone.
Your wit, your bravery . . . and that young one
who spoke to you just now, she worshipped you.

CYRANO

The one with the milk jugs? Do you think that's true?
I've slept with girls: Roxane is something new.

DEBRAY

I watched Roxane grow pale during the fight;
she's half won over in her mind and heart.
Cheer up, old man; speak to her, make your case.

CYRANO

I'm terrified she'd laugh right in my face;
but look, her confidante, young Geneviève.

Enter GENEVIÈVE.

GENEVIÈVE

Monsieur . . . ? Monsieur de Bergerac, by your leave,
Roxane asked me to have a word with you
and organize a quiet rendezvous:
there's something important she wants to talk about.
Would ten o'clock in the morning be all right?

CYRANO

Of course; but where?

GENEVIÈVE

Oh, that's for you to say.

CYRANO

. . . Ragueneau's coffee shop in the rue St Honoré —
first thing tomorrow I'll be there, okay?

Exit GENEVIÈVE.

Did you hear that?

Now is your mind at peace?

CYRANO
(*shouts*)
At peace? No, I feel valorous and fierce.
I need giants to fight; I could win a war.

JODELET
Be quiet, you two; we're still rehearsing here!

Re-enter LIGNIÈRE *supported by commedia dell'arte figures.*

LIGNIÈRE
(*pathetically*)
I got this note . . . A hundred men in ambush —
my gossip column, you know; that shit de Guiche;
at the Porte de Nesle, between here and my flat.
Cyrano, can you put me up tonight?
If not, your old friend is as good as dead.

CYRANO
Lignière, tonight you'll sleep in your own bed.
(*to others*)
Take up those lights; no one need be afraid.

DEBRAY
You're going to risk our lives for this drunken sot?

CYRANO
Oh, stop complaining: certainly, why not?

Claps LIGNIÈRE *on the shoulder.*

This drunken sot, this ruin, this bin of wine
did something once I thought was truly fine:
seeing a girl he loved dabble her finger-tips

in holy water, he raised it to his lips
and drank it off like a trough of best Bordeaux,
he who had never much time for H_2O.

ACTRESS
Oh, but that's lovely.

CYRANO
Charming, don't you think?

ACTRESS
But why so many against a simple drunk?

CYRANO
. . . Okay, line up; and please, this is my row.
I want no interference from any of you.
Cast, stagehands, electricians, musicians too;
give us a tune on the fiddle and off we go.
Take up the lights; let's have a sprightly air:
I lead from the front; and remember, it's my war.
Everyone ready? Doorman, open the door!

Door opens to reveal a moonlit cityscape; music.

. . . Ah, Paris at night, adrift in a cloudy doze,
an enchanted fairyland where anything goes;
over her dreaming tiles the moonlight flows,
a perfect sound-stage for the coming scene.
Down there, wrapped in scarves of mist, the Seine,
a magic mirror bright with moonlit mystery,
trembles; and we shall see what we shall see.

Commedia dell'arte figures, MUSICIANS *etc form an excited
group on the threshold.*

. . . You ask why so many men against one poor hack?
He's an old friend of Cyrano de Bergerac
and that's more reason than enough, dear girl.

43

ALL

To the Porte de Nesle! . . . de Nesle! The Porte de Nesle!

RAGUENEAU's *bakery and coffee shop; morning. Books, magazines.*
RAGUENEAU, BAKERS; LIZ RAGUENEAU *chats aside with an* OFFICER.
RAGUENEAU *writes and stops.*

RAGUENEAU
(*soliloquizes*)
Ragueneau, silence the singing god within:
your pots and pans shine in the morning sun.
The verses later, first the cakes and pies —
lyrics and buns, both metaphors of heaven.
There's as much poetry in a well-made gâteau
as in all Rimbaud's *saisons et châteaux.*
Muse, off you go, lest your bewitching eyes
suffer the thick smoke of my blazing oven.
(*to* BAKER)
Remember to divide your loaves like mine:
place the caesura halfway through the line.

BAKER
(*presenting an edible lyre*)
Cher maître, I baked this over a low fire,
thinking it might amuse you.

RAGUENEAU
Orpheus' lyre!

BAKER
Puff pastry and dried fruit; spun-sugar strings.

RAGUENEAU
Excellent; thank you; the poor dough has wings.
. . . Liz, love, do you not think it's beautiful?

44

LIZ

The thing's absurd; sometimes you're such a fool.

RAGUENEAU

Bags, please . . . what, my colleagues' poetry papers
torn and divided up to make cake wrappers?
The Bacchae dismember Orpheus once more!

LIZ

Orpheus, indeed, what else would I use them for?
Even I could write better stuff if I chose.

RAGUENEAU

I hate to think what you would do with prose.

Enter CYRANO, *a bundle of nerves, his hand bandaged.*

CYRANO

What's the time?

RAGUENEAU

Ten to ten.

CYRANO

Ten minutes to go.

RAGUENEAU

I saw your fight in the theatre: what a show!
'With the final line . . . '

CYRANO

What's the time, Ragueneau?

RAGUENEAU

Five-to.

CYRANO

A lady will be arriving soon;
we need to talk for half an hour alone.

45

But the poetry group is coming here at ten.

CYRANO
Well, shove them down the back. Have you got a pen?
(*aside*)
. . . My nerves are wrecked, I can't go through with it;
the quill is quivering as I try to write.
I'll take my leave, first giving her this note,
a love-letter I've rewritten time after time,
into her hand; no need to sign my name.

Enter POETS, *famished and excitable.*

1ST POET
We were stopped at the Porte de Nesle by a huge crowd:
a dozen corpses stretched out in the mud,
flick-knives and chains lying all over the road.

2ND POET
They say one man, a single man, put paid
to the whole bunch . . .

3RD POET
. . . and meanwhile scared the shite
from dozens more who fled into the night
scattering in confusion left and right
to sob in dingy pubs, their faces white.

4TH POET
Abandoned hats were found in the place Dauphine,
the quai de Conti, the rue Mazarine,
even St Michel . . .

RAGUENEAU
Do we know who he is?

1ST POET
Some lion-heart for sure.

CYRANO
(*aside*)
'Your lips, your eyes;
I faint with awe when you materialize.'

The POETS *help themselves to buns and drinks.*

2ND POET
(*to* RAGUENEAU)
Any new poems, *maître*?

RAGUENEAU
Not really, no;
a recipe in verse.

3RD POET
Let's hear it though.

4TH POET
(*tasting*)
Scrumptious!

1ST POET
(*munching*)
We're listening.

2ND POET
(*drinking*)
Mmmm, you warm our hearts.

RAGUENEAU
(*strikes an attitude*)
. . . 'A Recipe in Verse for Almond Tarts':
To make my almond tarts,
One of the finer arts,
I whip up a white froth
While introducing both
A crush of almond paste
And a squeeze of lemon zest.

I stuff the mix with care
Into these cake-moulds here.
Apricot glaze to taste,
Or peach if you prefer;
Then, careful not to trip
And screw the whole thing up,
I place the gold confection
With infinite affection
In a pre-heated stove
Or even a microwave
Until the crisping starts:
Ragueneau's Almond Tarts!

3RD POET
(*choking*)

Delicious.

4TH POET
Exquisite; try these savoury buns.

CYRANO
Ragueneau, can't you see your poet friends
are scoffing everything with their bare hands?

RAGUENEAU
Of course I see, but I ignore the sight
since noticing might spoil their appetite.
Besides, their visits give me a special treat:
with them for an audience I get to recite
my poems, the undernourished get to eat,
and bread is poetry to a grumbling gut.

CYRANO
(*claps him on the shoulder*)
Perhaps; in any case you've a generous heart.
. . . Liz, is this officer offering you advances?

LIZ
Oh, I know how to order my defences.

48

CYRANO
Yet he carries himself with a victorious air.
Your husband is my friend; please treat him fair.

LIZ
· (*to* OFFICER)
You're a fine one; you should have come to blows:
why didn't you punch him on the nose?

OFFICER
The *nose* . . . ?

Exit LIZ *and* OFFICER; *enter* GENEVIÈVE *and* ROXANE.

CYRANO
Geneviève, do you like buns and chocolate cake?
Here, help yourself and take them down the back.
(*to* ROXANE)
A moment to be treasured, yes indeed . . .
something that couldn't wait, I think you said?

ROXANE
But first a warm word of appreciation
for putting that grim idiot out of action,
the one de Guiche, who wants me, tries to make . . .

CYRANO
A complaisant spouse? Oh yes, I know that trick;
so much the better if the rascal dies;
I fought, then, not for my nose but your bright eyes?

ROXANE
. . . And saved me from two odious *liaisons*.
I want to ask . . . but, before I give my reason,
I need to re-imagine that childhood cousin
I played with in the park, beside the lake . . .

CYRANO
Those summers you used to spend at Bergerac.

49

ROXANE

Castle and cloud-shadow as in a story-book,
river and rocky meadow to the horizon;
you made toy swords with reeds from the lake-shore.

CYRANO

Wheat from the fields provided your dolls with hair.

ROXANE

Games in the forest; babes in the wood . . .

CYRANO

The heat
of a silent barn; hide and seek; ripening fruit.

ROXANE

You'd do what I ordered without a second thought.

CYRANO

You in short skirts.

ROXANE

Was I pretty?

CYRANO

Hmm, pretty enough.

ROXANE

Sometimes in your mad games, if you'd been rough,
you'd run to me, pretending to be tough,
with a hand scratched from climbing; playing nurse,
I'd scold you in my severest tone of voice:
'Have you been fighting with the bigger boys?'

She takes his hand.

. . . What's this? I don't believe it. Hold it out . . .
at your age; and how did this come about?

CYRANO

Still fighting with the big boys, don't you know.
You hold my hand just as you used to do.

ROXANE

How many of them?

CYRANO

A hundred or so, no more.
Never mind that, but tell me why you're here.

ROXANE

It's strange the strength old memories can revive;
so now I can speak frankly. I'm in love:
someone who doesn't know about it yet,
who looks at me but doesn't speak his thought
though I can see he'd like to be my lover.
No, here, give me your hand; you have a fever.
Here, let me clean it with a piece of lint;
I'll tie you a new bandage if you want . . .
. . . A young cadet in your own regiment,
clever and proud, courageous, handsome too . . .
You're pale and shivering; what's wrong with you?

CYRANO

It's this damned cut.

ROXANE

Here, take a drink of water.
I've only glimpsed him at the theatre.

CYRANO

You haven't spoken?

ROXANE

Only in silent glances;
but people talk, and my acquaintances . . .

CYRANO

Tell me his name.

ROXANE

Christian de Neuchâteau.

CYRANO

I've never heard of him, is he someone new?

ROXANE

He starts this morning with Castel-Jaloux.

CYRANO

Roxane, you're a bright girl: your art, your books.
What if this boy has nothing but his looks?
He may be a dope, illiterate, stupid, dull . . .

ROXANE

No, he's like the young prince in a fairy tale.

CYRANO

. . . a handsome moron.

ROXANE

No, I know he's not.

CYRANO

But if he is?

ROXANE

I'd drop dead on the spot.

CYRANO

And what has all this got to do with me?

ROXANE

Most of your comrades are from Gascony . . .

CYRANO

. . . and you're afraid we'd victimize some proud
youngster signed up, through influence, in our crowd?

ROXANE

Yes.

CYRANO

Not without reason.

ROXANE

But you came on
so strong last night, transfixing everyone . . .

CYRANO

Don't fret, I'll keep an eye on the young man.

ROXANE

You and I were always a special couple,
such friends.

CYRANO

Of course.

ROXANE

You'll keep him out of trouble?

CYRANO

I swear.

ROXANE

I love you; now I must fly . . . Christian:
tell him to write to me . . . A *hundred* men?
You haven't told me about this famous fight
you fought with the big boys again last night.
Another time. I love you: what magnificence!

ROXANE *blows him a kiss and exits.*

CYRANO

Oh, that was nothing; I've been braver since.

Enter JALOUX, *older than* CYRANO, *good-natured and protective of his* CADETS.

RAGUENEAU

Good morning, Captain de Castel-Jaloux.

JALOUX

Good morning, monsieur Ragueneau, how d'you do?
... Cyrano, are you there? We heard the news.
Half the cadets are here, out in the mews,
toasting you at the Bar Palais-Royal,
tongues hanging out to hear your gory tale.

CYRANO *declines;* JALOUX *shouts to* CADETS *off.*

The man's too shy today; he wants to hide!
... They're coming over, with a delirious crowd;
the whole neighbourhood is wild with ecstasy.

Enter CADETS (BILL, JULES *etc*), *a startlingly animated bunch.*

CADETS

Uasal; scéiniúil; spreagúil; álainn; aobhinn!
Commendious; bontious; grantious; galantine!

RAGUENEAU

You are all Gascons?

CADETS
Yes, but don't be scared.

RAGUENEAU

Help yourselves to the coffee and China tea,
the buns, the biscuits and my special cakes,
but mind the magazines; don't touch the books!
Good heavens, what have we here? *Le tout Paris!*

Enter MARQUIS, JOURNALIST, DEBRAY *and curious* SPECTATORS.

MARQUIS
(*to* CYRANO)
I've a coach, sir, with certain ladies in it
who'd like to meet you if you have a minute.

JOURNALIST
(*to* CYRANO)
Théophraste Renaudot, sir, of the *Gazette*:
can you let me have some details about last night?

DEBRAY
Everything now becomes a tabloid feature;
they say the idea has a tremendous future.
. . . Cyrano, are you in pain? What's wrong with you?

Enter DE GUICHE.

DE GUICHE
Good morning, Captain de Castel-Jaloux . . .
(*to* CYRANO)
. . . I'm here with my congratulations too;
your sudden fame has struck my uncle Richelieu.
You serve with the Gascon space cadets, I hear?

CYRANO
Yes, with these noble gentlemen you see here.

JALOUX
Since you're the bright star of the regiment,
Cyrano, please present them to the Count.

CYRANO
(*politely*)
These are the Gascon Cadets
Of Captain de Castel-Jaloux,
Notorious liars and cheats,
A palaeolithic zoo;

55

Paternity suits and debts,
They never stand in a queue.

These are as good as it gets;
Their knuckles brush the dew.
Proud of their guts and threats,
Full of their own ballyhoo,
They'd give you a clash in the slats
As quick as they'd look at you.

Grinning like wolves or cats,
These are the special few,
Ostriches in their shabby hats
In case the holes show through;
Old Fenians and Jacobites,
They are poets and dreamers too.

They love to get into fights
Or a bit of old *parlez-vous*.
Christ, what a bunch of shits,
What an unspeakable crew.
Such are the Gascon Cadets
Of Captain de Castel-Jaloux.

DE GUICHE
(*amused*)
It's fashionable these days to have a poet.
If I offered you a position would you do it?
Your style intrigues my uncle Richelieu;
I could put in a word with him for you.
Have you written a play? He's a great theatre-goer
and would change only a line or two, I'm sure.

CYRANO
I'd turn to ice if anyone changed a line
or altered a comma in anything of mine.

DE GUICHE
Work that he likes he generously rewards.

CYRANO

My best reward is the truth of my own words.

DE GUICHE

You're proud.

CYRANO

You've noticed?

Enter more CADETS *with hats stuck on a sword.*

CADET

　　　　　　　Look, some fragrant fluff
those game-birds left behind when they ran off.
What are we going to do with this ripe bunch?
Perhaps they could be boiled in a pot for lunch.

RAGUENEAU

Whoever paid them for that act of treachery
can't be too pleased this morning.

DE GUICHE

　　　　　　　That was me.
I hired them to chastise a scribbling drunk —
hardly a task for one of my social rank.

CYRANO

Perhaps you would return these to your friends?

DE GUICHE

(coldly)

My coach waits; here our conversation ends.
You've read *Quixote*?

CYRANO

Certainly I have
and feel a kinship with the old psychopath.

DE GUICHE

The windmills; you remember how he goes . . . ?

CYRANO

Chapter eight. Do you mean I pick my foes
from those who swing with every wind that blows?

DE GUICHE

The mill of fortune, with its revolving oars,
could cast you into the mud.

CYRANO

Or among the stars.

Exit DE GUICHE.

DEBRAY

And so, your chance to be a distinguished poet
vanishes once again; you overdo it.

CYRANO

Of course I overdo it; but on principle
and as an example to more timorous people.

DEBRAY

If you could modify your usual course,
fame and fortune . . .

CYRANO

But there's nothing worse!
I pick a powerful sponsor, lick his arse
and rise by stealth instead of my own force
like ivy crawling up a rotten branch?
No, thank you. Raise funds like the usual bunch
by spouting received wisdom? Act the clown
to please some fashionable art tycoon
who pays the piper, therefore calls the tune?
Ingratiate myself with the academy,
do daily push-ups for the bourgeoisie?

No, thank you. Make a point of imitation,
suiting my style to the most recent fashion,
ironically of course? No, thank you; better
an unknown rarity than a crowd-pleasing writer.
Grace nouveau houses with my honest poetry,
the cynosure of a slick coterie?
Suck up to editors and opinion makers
to win prizes devised by corporate jokers?
Discover genius only in the trite
and live in fear of journalistic spite?
Be wretched if my innovative lines
go unremarked in the best magazines?
No, cheap ambition's never been my thing,
celebrity, influence; but to dream, to sing,
to laugh, write as I please and act from choice
with a clear eye and my own distinctive voice;
at the very least to strike out with panache,
amaze a gaping audience, cut a dash
and fight for my convictions, not for cash
and fame, but for uncontaminated air;
to fly alone, even to the moon up there.
Do you not see the virtue in being rude?
I'm sick and tired of the prescribed attitude.
I write nothing that doesn't come from the heart
so I can say, sincerely on my part,
I'm satisfied with the modest flowers I find,
knowing they've grown in my own patch of ground;
then, if at last I win some recognition,
it's not the result of a base calculation
since I take pride in the thing for its own sake.
I'm not the ivy clinging to the bark
but the trunk itself: no venerable elm
or oak, perhaps, but prince in my own realm.

DEBRAY

Okay, but why the confrontational air?
How did you contract this mad desire
to turn people against you everywhere?

CYRANO

By watching all your mediocre cronies
busily making up to the other phonies.
I like to be difficult, and often smile
to think, 'Another enemy for my file.'
Perversity? Yes indeed, I must admit
displeasing is my pleasure; I love their hate.
Can you imagine how my spirits rise
under the firing-line of their furious eyes?
I get a kick from the vindictive spite
of cowards, the envious and the second-rate.
You take things as they come, live and let live,
but I prefer to be more positive.
Daily hostility keeps my backbone straight,
my nerves receptive and my head upright —
a pain in the neck that makes a man stand out
like a stiff collar on a floppy shirt.
As for the nose, I'd sooner lose my dick;
besides, the women like it when I lick . . .

DEBRAY

Put a bold front on it, but face the fact
you love her and she doesn't love you back.

Enter CHRISTIAN, *who picks up a magazine.*

BILL
(*to* CYRANO)

Aren't you going to tell us now about the fight?
It'll be an education for this new recruit,
this shy beginner who's come here to train
from, where is it, some northern place: Touraine.

JULES
(*to* CHRISTIAN)

Young northerner, a quick word in your ear:
there's one feature we never mention here.

CHRISTIAN

You mean his . . . ?

PATRICK

Shhh; the word is never said —
he flattened two men with the flu because
he thought they were laughing at his famous . . . toes.

BRIAN

Unless you wish to die you'd best avoid
mention of membrane, sinus and adenoid.

HUGH

Take out a handkerchief and you draw your shroud.

The CADETS *stare silently at* CHRISTIAN.

CHRISTIAN

Captain, how do I deal with this valiant crew?

JALOUX

Show them a northerner can be valiant too.

GUS

And now, the fight; the fight!

CYRANO

The fight? Here goes.

ALL *sit;* CHRISTIAN *straddles a chair apart.*

. . . Backed by some friends, I step out on my own.
High in the night sky hangs a radiant moon
white as a clock-face when, to my surprise,
a bank of cloud obscures the summer skies.
Darkness descends as on a winter night;
the quays are silent, not a soul in sight.
It's late; the lights are out; the darkness grows;
I can't see any farther than (*my hand*) . . .

CHRISTIAN
(*loud and clear*)
Your nose.

Sensation; all slowly rise, their eyes on CYRANO; *a pause.*

CYRANO
(*stupefied*)
Who is that man?

JACQUES
He starts with us today.
Christian de Neuchâteau.

CYRANO
(*controls himself*)
. . . Okay; okay.
As I was saying — Jesus! — it was dark.

ALL *sit again.*

Though rather fearing, for a drunkard's sake,
I shall displease some eminence who can wreck . . .

CHRISTIAN
Your nose.

ALL *rise again.*

CYRANO
. . . my future chances of promotion,
I think — Christ! — of my valorous reputation
when all at once, out of the misty shadows,
a filthy ruffian grabs me by . . .

CHRISTIAN
The nose.

CYRANO

. . . the shoulder; but I dump him in the muck.
More scum; I run them through; they swing; I duck.
Whirling about, what do I find?

CHRISTIAN

Who knows?

CYRANO

I'm face to face with dozens.

CHRISTIAN

Nose to nose.

CYRANO

I charge, head down, not taking time to pause,
and catching several in the . . .

CHRISTIAN
Nose.

CYRANO

. . . the jaws.
I'm winning . . .

CHRISTIAN

By a nose.

CYRANO

(*gasping*)
No, by a head:
some half a dozen are already dead,
so help me . . . Just as their line begins to break
one rabbit-punches me in the . . .

CHRISTIAN

Nose.

CYRANO

                                   . . . the neck.
God damn it, clear the shop before I crack!

Exit all except CYRANO *and* CHRISTIAN.

. . . Give me your hand.

                    CHRISTIAN
                    My hand?

                    CYRANO
                              Yes, I'm her cousin.

                    CHRISTIAN
Whose cousin?

                    CYRANO
          Why, Roxane's.

                    CHRISTIAN
                              So that's the reason;
she's told you . . .

                    CYRANO
          Yes.

                    CHRISTIAN
                    She likes me? Are you sure?
Well, I'm honoured to make your acquaintance, sir.
I apologize for the noses.

                    CYRANO
                    They don't matter.
Some time soon, though, she expects a letter . . .

                    CHRISTIAN
Damn.

CYRANO
What's the problem?

CHRISTIAN
Everything's all right
till I open my stupid mouth or try to write;
I get so tongue-tied I could die of fright.

CYRANO
You're bright enough to know you're not so bright;
and the noses showed you can be pretty quick.

CHRISTIAN
Schoolboy stuff; with women I'm not so slick.
I blush like a child; their beauty strikes me dumb.

CYRANO
They're just like us, though, as you'll learn in time.

CHRISTIAN
I adore them, but I don't know how to speak.

CYRANO
I do; but look at this unromantic beak.

CHRISTIAN
If only I could become an eloquent rogue.

CYRANO
(aside)
And I a young buck with a handsome mug.

CHRISTIAN
Clever herself, she'll take me for a fool.

CYRANO
(aside)
With looks like those I could reveal my soul.

CHRISTIAN

I've no gift of the gab.

CYRANO
(*abruptly*)
. . . So, why don't I lend you mine?
With your looks and my brains we're bound to win;
together we'll make a first-rate leading man.
Do you think you could learn my speeches line for line?
Don't fret, between us we won't let her down
if the soft heart behind this monstrous form
speaks through your noble brow and obvious charm.

CHRISTIAN
You're very keen on this idea, aren't you?

CYRANO
Indeed I am . . . Well, it would be fun to do,
the kind of exercise that tempts a poet —
ventriloquism, romance; so, shall we try it?
I think of it as a commissioned task
with me your voice and you my handsome mask.

CHRISTIAN
But the letter she expects . . .

CYRANO
(*takes out his letter to* ROXANE)
Look, here it is;
we're always scribbling something to the Muse.
This will be just the thing, you can be sure;
all it requires is your own signature.
We carry in our pockets at all times
odd thoughts, phrases and images, lists of rhymes;
for ever blowing bubbles in the air,
we dream up ideal women everywhere.
So, change its fictions to realities. Here:
a note as lyrical as it's insincere.

CHRISTIAN

But won't it need a bit of a re-write?
Dashed off at random, how can it relate . . . ?

CYRANO

Everything's serious to a girl in love;
believe me, it will fit her like a glove.
Roxane, beguiled by its importunate tone,
will think those words were written for her alone.

CHRISTIAN
(*embraces* CYRANO)

My friend!

Re-enter tentative CADETS; *also* LIZ *and* OFFICER.

CYRANO

My brother; we shall act as one.

BILL

Dead silence; I can hardly bear to look.

JALOUX

Get out of the way and let me have a peek.
. . . The dear man is as peaceful as an apostle:
strike one nostril, he turns the other nostril.

OFFICER
(*showing off to* LIZ)

Can we mention his nose now? Do you think it's safe?
. . . Hey, Cyrano, what's that frightful stink?

CYRANO
(*sends him flying*)
Fuck off!

General relief.

Old square, evening; doors left and right; RAGUENEAU, GENEVIÈVE.

RAGUENEAU
. . . and then she left me for another man.
I hanged myself, being bankrupt and alone,
but Cyrano came in; he cut me down
and fixed me up as a butler to Roxane.

GENEVIÈVE
But how do you explain your misadventure?

RAGUENEAU
My wife liked soldiers and not literature.

RAGUENEAU *exits to house.*

GENEVIÈVE
(*calls*)
Roxane? Roxane, come on, it's nearly six!
We'll miss that lecture on 'The Art of Sex'.

ROXANE *appears on balcony.*

ROXANE
Coming. My God, are they going to serenade us?

Enter CYRANO *with* MUSICIANS.

CYRANO
I, Cyrano, an admirer of all ladies,
devoted as you know to things uncommon,
am here to honour two exceptional women,
roses and laurels, with my usual brio.
The musicians will now play for you in stereo.

MUSICIANS *sing, their instruments now electrified.*

On gleaming linen spread
In an enormous bed,

Above our heads a knot
Of twined forget-me-not,
We two shall sleep as one
Till life itself be done,
Till life itself be done.

GENEVIÈVE
Who are these daft rockers you've brought along?

CYRANO
(*to* MUSICIANS)
Go on, get lost; sing Montfleury a song;
make it discordant, vicious and very long.

Exit MUSICIANS.

. . . I'm here tonight, as I am every other,
to ask Roxane about her witty lover.

Enter ROXANE.

ROXANE
He's wittier daily, so warm and articulate;
even wittier than yourself.

CYRANO
You may be right.

ROXANE
No one but he could be so sensitive
to those nuances which are the soul of love.
Words fail him sometimes, and he's in disgrace;
then he says things that make my pulses race.

CYRANO
I don't believe it.

ROXANE
Men are all like you:

being fair of face, he must be stupid too?

CYRANO
He speaks from great imaginative resources?

ROXANE
Not only speaks; he positively discourses.

CYRANO
And writes?

ROXANE
(*takes out a letter*)
How about this? 'The more of love
you take from me the more I have to give.'
Or: 'Since I require a strong heart that endures,
and you have mine, be sure to send me yours.'

CYRANO
His heart is empty, next it overflows:
how much heart does he need, do you suppose?

ROXANE
You're jealous.

CYRANO
Jealous?

ROXANE
Of his graceful prose:
(*recites by heart*)
'I seal my kisses in these envelopes,
so read what I write to you with murmuring lips.'

CYRANO
Now that's not bad . . . if no great work of art.
So you know all his letters off by heart?
That's real appreciation and no mistake.

ROXANE

He's brilliant.

CYRANO

Brilliant?

ROXANE

Brilliant!

CYRANO
(*modestly*)
Oh, if you like.

Enter DE GUICHE.

ROXANE

De Guiche! Hide; for the sight of you with me
could put him on the scent of our conspiracy.
He wants me for himself; he mustn't know;
he could make trouble for us if he wanted to.

CYRANO *hides.*

DE GUICHE

I've come to take my leave.

ROXANE
I'm just going out;

you're off?

DE GUICHE
Yes, for the war, this very night.
I've papers ordering us to the siege of Metz.
My departure causes you no great regrets?
It saddens me, the thought of our separation.
I've been appointed colonel, for the duration,
of the regiment where your noisy cousin serves;
I'll see that he gets the treatment he deserves.

ROXANE
(*aside*)
. . . Christian . . .

DE GUICHE
What's wrong?

ROXANE
I'm overcome with fear
since someone I like so much is going to war.

DE GUICHE
Your first kind word to me, on the day I go.

ROXANE
You're going to take revenge on Cyrano?

DE GUICHE
You're on his side?

ROXANE
Not necessarily so.

DE GUICHE
Do you see him often?

ROXANE
Only when I have to.

DE GUICHE
One sees him everywhere with what's-his-name,
that new cadet, the stupid one.

ROXANE
Oh, him . . .
Your plan for Cyrano isn't very subtle
if you aim to place him in the line of battle:
what if the regiment went off to the war
without him and his cadets, leaving him here

kicking his heels in town, mad with frustration?
If you really want to drive him to distraction
keep him and the others here safe from the action.
He'll eat his heart out, far from the line of fire,
and you'll have all the vengeance you require.

                    DE GUICHE
Only a woman could think of such a plan:
do you really like me a little bit, Roxane?
Can I take this as a sign of love?

                    ROXANE
                    You can.

                    DE GUICHE
I've orders here for each of the companies,
effective from tonight; except for these,
the cadets', which I shall keep for my own eyes.
De Bergerac and his vainglorious dreams!
Even you can play a trick or two?

                    ROXANE
                    Sometimes.

                    DE GUICHE
My dear, you set my senses in a whirl;
I'll visit you tonight, fantastic girl.
Although I'm ordered to the front at once
I can't abandon this amazing chance.
The Capuchin priory in the rue d'Orléans
will put me up for a few hours before dawn;
it will be thought that I've already gone.
I'll come masked so nobody will know
and spend, if I may, one night before I go.

                    ROXANE
If this gets out — your name, your reputation . . .

DE GUICHE

Don't worry; I can handle the situation.

ROXANE

I'm asking you to go while the rest remain;
I want you to be a great hero, Antoine.

DE GUICHE

You've never used my Christian name before.
Give me an hour or so; don't lock the door.

Exit DE GUICHE.

ROXANE

Really, monsieur de Guiche: no bloody fear!
                    (*to* GENEVIÈVE)
Ginny, let's go and catch 'The Art of Sex';
and not a word to Cyrano, d'you hear?
He mustn't know I robbed him of his war.

Re-enter CYRANO.

                    (*to* CYRANO)
Tell Christian I'll be back in a few ticks;
I want to hear him talk about love and passion
in an inspired, extemporaneous fashion.
Don't warn him though; he must be unprepared.

CYRANO

Of course; good Lord!

ROXANE
            Shh!

CYRANO
            Shh!

ROXANE
                    Shh! Not a word.

Exit ROXANE *and* GENEVIÈVE; *enter* CHRISTIAN.

CYRANO

Christian, take out your amatory notebooks;
you're going to distinguish yourself on this occasion.

CHRISTIAN

No.

CYRANO

No? What's wrong? You have to get by heart . . .

CHRISTIAN

I'm tired of borrowing your superior art,
of playing a role and shaking with stage-fright.
It was fine at first, and thank you for your advice,
but the time has come to speak with my own voice.

CYRANO
(*sceptically*)

Okay.

CHRISTIAN

What makes you think I don't know how?
I'm not so stupid, as you'll discover now.
I've learnt from your invaluable instruction
and now I can speak up without constriction.
I'll hold her in my arms tonight for sure.

Re-enter ROXANE *and* PRÉCIEUSES.

. . . God, here she comes; don't leave me alone with her!

CYRANO

No, no, extemporize; you're perfectly right.
Speak for yourself, don't let me interfere.

ROXANE

Aurélia, 'Lumineuse, Garance, goodnight.

Exit PRÉCIEUSES.

GENEVIÈVE
I'm going home too and I think I'll walk:
too bad we were so late for the sexy talk.

Exit GENEVIÈVE; CYRANO *hides.*

ROXANE
. . . Christian, it's you. It's starting to get dark —
so quiet, so peaceful; nobody in the park.
The rest have gone; sit here in this alcove.
What's on your mind?

CHRISTIAN
(*after a pause*)
I'm thinking about love.

ROXANE
(*closes her eyes*)
Oh, speak of love. You love me, yes — the premise;
go on from there; expatiate.

CHRISTIAN
I promise
to love you, and I'd like you to love me too.
Roxane, can you not show me that you do?

ROXANE
You give me yoghurt when I ask for cream;
be fluent.

CHRISTIAN
I think about you all the time.

ROXANE
Elaborate a little, for heavens' sake!

CHRISTIAN

Would it be okay if I kissed your neck?

ROXANE

No, I don't think so, idiot; you're a disgrace,
more so than if you had an ugly face.
You'd better smarten up and quickly, brother;
go home and get your stupid head together
or we can drop the idea of real relations.

CHRISTIAN

Roxane, I love you . . .

ROXANE

So, congratulations.

Exit to house; re-enter CYRANO.

CHRISTIAN

You've got to help me put this right, and soon.

CYRANO

How am I to do that, you hopeless clown?

Light appears in ROXANE's *upstairs window.*

CHRISTIAN

Look!

CYRANO

Her window . . . shh, keep your voice down.
It's not the end of the world. A cloudy sky . . .
You don't deserve it, but it's worth a try.
Stand there, under the balcony; I'll hide here
and prompt you from the shadows. Can you hear?

Re-enter MUSICIANS.

MUSICIANS
We've just been serenading Montfleury.

CYRANO
There's something more you lot can do for me —
one at each end of the street; you here, you there.
If anyone comes strike up a tune.

MUSICIANS
What tune?

CYRANO
Light-hearted for a woman, grim for a man.

Exit MUSICIANS.

. . . Call her.

CHRISTIAN
Roxane!

CYRANO
We have to throw a pebble.

He throws; ROXANE *appears on balcony.*

ROXANE
Who's there?

CHRISTIAN
It's Christian.

ROXANE
You're despicable.
Your clichés leave me cold, you're too much trouble;
and you don't love me, you inarticulate bore.

CHRISTIAN
(*whom* CYRANO *prompts from the shadows*)
I'm dumb because I love you more and more.
I've never loved anyone like this before;
I'm tongue-tied because I'm so sincere.
My love grows stronger by the day, the hour,
like a cherubic infant in its cot.
Originally no more than a tiny tot,
it glows and babbles; I can hear it roar!

ROXANE
(*about to shut the window, hesitates*)
That's better; tell me more about this child.

CHRISTIAN
(*as before*)
It howls and stretches — tremulous, and wild!

ROXANE
(*leans out*)
Why are you speaking with such hesitant pauses?
Does your mind operate in paraphrases?

CYRANO
(*to* CHRISTIAN)
This is too tricky; let me take it from here.
(*to* ROXANE *in a strained voice*)
. . . It's dark; my words are trying to find your ear
like a bee fumbling at a half-open flower.

ROXANE
(*re-opens the window*)
My own have no such problem; *you* can hear.

CYRANO
Because they fly directly to my heart.
My heart so vast, your ear so intricate,
your words pour down like moon-water, while mine
climb to your balcony like a twining vine.

ROXANE
(*steps on to balcony*)
They're climbing faster than a minute ago.

CYRANO
They've grown light-headed from this vertigo.

ROXANE
Do I speak to you from such an enormous height?

CYRANO
You do; don't drop a harsh word on my heart.

ROXANE
I'm coming down.

CYRANO
No!

ROXANE
Climb up on the bench;
grab hold of a drainpipe and a jasmine branch.

CYRANO
No, no; let's take advantage of the night
to whisper without the material blaze of sight.

ROXANE
Blindly?

CYRANO
Not blindly; I can just make you out.
You see the dark shape of a trailing cloak,
I the faint glimmer of a summer frock.
Me a mere shadow, you a radiant gleam,
I talk to you now as in a waking dream.
If only I were eloquent . . .

ROXANE
But you are.

CYRANO
I've never opened my heart like this before.
I quailed beneath your gaze, but now I seem
to be able to speak to you for the first time.

ROXANE
You certainly seem to speak with a new inflection.

CYRANO
I think I do; for, under the protection
of darkness, I could . . . Please forgive this hesitancy:
it's so delicious, and so new for me
to find the courage to expose my soul,
I who am always scared of others' ridicule.

ROXANE
Ridicule?

CYRANO
Yes, I'd rather be shy than smart;
a foolish diffidence constrains my heart.
I reach for a star; then, from a morbid dread
of ridicule, I pluck a flower instead.

ROXANE
What's wrong with flowers?

CYRANO
No flowers; not now, not here.

ROXANE
You've never spoken to me like this before.

CYRANO
If we could once forget the conventional things,
the roses, the pierced hearts, the fairy wings,

and get to something larger, something true;
instead of sipping from exhausted springs
to drink from the full river in its flow.

And wit?

		Wit now would be to insult the night,
nature itself, the jasmine scent, the moonlight;
one glimpse of the heavens and their infinite spaces
reveals the absurdity of our artifices.
What scares me is that the alchemy we share
may fail to distil true love, the real, the rare,
wasting its time on fanciful pastimes
while our sophistication destroys our dreams.

And poetry?

		We've had too many love poems,
too much of posturing, badinage, word games.
I pity those who are untouched by it
but once in a lifetime, maybe, the moment comes
for a true, noble love beyond sport and wit,
beyond flashy metaphors; one which bewails
each fine phrase for the tragedy it conceals.

If this once-in-a-lifetime moment is now at hand,
what words appropriate to it can we decently find?

What words I have at my command are yours;
I scatter them before you like wildflowers
in their wild state, not tied up in a wreath.
I'm mad with love for you; I can hardly breathe.
Your name sleeps like a wind-chime in my heart;

whenever I hear 'Roxane' the chime rings out.
I cherish everything you do or say:
last month, for instance, on the fourth of May,
you changed your hairstyle before going out.
To me your hair has been the soul of light
and, just as when we gaze at the sunrise
gold sun-spots dance thereafter in our eyes
so, turning from the bright blaze you inspire,
my dazzled vision finds you everywhere.

ROXANE
(*moved*)

Yes, this is love.

CYRANO

        It shakes me to the core,
kind and ferocious, with a fierce desire,
a wild anxiety and consuming fire;
and yet there's nothing egotistical here. .
I'd gladly give my happiness for your own
even if, to you, the fact remained unknown —
if only, at a distance, once or twice
I'd hear your laugh, thanks to my sacrifice.
Each time you look at me, or I at you,
I'm filled with renewed valour, renewed virtue.
Do you understand? Do you feel my worship rise,
here in the darkness, to your shining eyes?
It's too much; can you imagine my delight
to know you're listening to all this tonight?
Even in my wildest dreams I didn't dare
hope we might have a moment like this to share.
Do my words touch your heart in the purple eaves?
You're shaking like a leaf among the leaves
and the adorable trembling of your hand
shivers the jasmine branches where I stand.

ROXANE

Yes, and I'm crying; I love you, mind and body.

83

CYRANO

Now death can come for me when it is ready:
blissful myself, have I inspired this bliss?
I ask for only one thing more . . .

CHRISTIAN
A kiss!

ROXANE

A kiss?

CHRISTIAN
A kiss.

CYRANO
(*whispers to* CHRISTIAN)
A kiss? You're going too quick!

CHRISTIAN
Now she's so moved, this is the time to strike.

CYRANO
(*to* ROXANE)
Perhaps you're still unwilling to be kissed;
forgive my nerve.

ROXANE
You mean you don't insist?

CYRANO
I'm too importunate; let's say no more.

CHRISTIAN
Why not?

CYRANO
Shut up!

ROXANE

What are you muttering for?

CYRANO

(*aside*)

Sooner or later it will have to occur,
the magic moment when the mouths concur
and the heads swim . . .

(*to* ROXANE)

Roxane, are you still there?
Already, darling, without noticing it,
you've left behind the exigencies of wit
and slipped from smiles to sighs, from sighs to tears.
Don't vex yourself with these irrational fears.
Having slipped already, you can slip some more;
from tears to kisses lies an open door.
Do you understand the significance of a kiss?
It's the embowerment of a loved face,
a gift more closely given, a more precise
promise, a token of what is still to come,
the pit and pith, a silent honeycomb,
a secret for the lips, not for the ears,
an infinity of briefly buzzing stars
in the plant-textured, moist interior,
the private eucharist of a crimson flower,
a warm glade where love can tell its truth
and drink the hot soul from the open mouth.

ROXANE

So climb up here and let me taste your breath,
this secret gift, this promise, this pit and pith.

CHRISTIAN

(*to* CYRANO)

Perhaps, after all, the moment is not yet right.

CYRANO

Go on, boy, get up there and do your stuff . . .

CHRISTIAN *climbs to* ROXANE; *they kiss.*

. . . On my wrung heart a fierce twinge, a dead weight:
love's feast, and I a Lazarus at the gate,
my only crumb that in this flowery dark
the words she kisses are the words I spoke.

Discordant music.

. . . Light-hearted; also grim: are the buggers drunk?
A man? A woman? Oh, I see; a monk:
Diogenes in search of an honest man.

Enter CAPUCHIN *with lantern,* ROXANE *and* CHRISTIAN *from house.*

CAPUCHIN

I've a letter here for a madame Roxane.
A spiritual question, I've no doubt:
a great lord asked me to deliver it.

CYRANO

De Guiche: is there no escape from the pompous twit?

ROXANE

De Guiche? Is the ruffian writing to me again?
(*Reads aside*) . . . 'The drums are beating; my own regiment
is due to leave this evening for the front.
They think I've gone ahead but I'm still here
at the monastery I mentioned; a simple friar
will place this letter in your gentle hand.
I'll see you later — alone, you understand —
and hope to pursue our new relations further.
Please don't disappoint your devoted . . .'
                    (*to* CAPUCHIN)
                                        Brother,
listen: 'Whether it pleases us or no,
we must obey my uncle Richelieu; so
into your dutiful hands I send this note

with a good friar, intelligent and discreet,
from the Capuchin priory in the next street.
Since my rich uncle maintains this priory,
please give my instructions absolute priority.
It is my personal wish that the friar perform
an immediate marriage in your own drawing-room:
yourself and Christian, whom I also send.
Even if you don't like him, be resigned
and try to treat him gently. Bear in mind
this must be done at once. The heavenly powers
will sing their praise of your obedience. Yours . . . '

CAPUCHIN *looks in puzzlement from* CHRISTIAN *to* CYRANO.

. . . A postscript: 'Give the church a thousand euros.'

CYRANO
Go on inside; get married; I'll mind the door.

Exit ROXANE, CHRISTIAN *and* CAPUCHIN *to house.*

. . . How to distract de Guiche for half an hour?

Grim music.

. . . A man all right . . . I know, I'll climb up here
if my presence doesn't disturb the atmosphere.

Climbs a tree; re-enter DE GUICHE *masked.*

DE GUICHE
Now where on earth is that pathetic friar?
This is the house; but who's this batman here?

CYRANO *drops; hidden face, funny voice.*

CYRANO
Where am I? What's the time? It's like a dream.
I fell straight from the moon like a moonbeam.

DE GUICHE

Oh yes? What kind of a lunatic are *you*?

CYRANO

How long my descent lasted I don't know.
A century or perhaps an hour ago
I was up there in that crocus-yellow sphere.
Where are we? Tell me frankly; have no fear.
Where have I landed like a meteorite?
I had no choice of my re-entry site.
Forgive me; sorry to give you such a shock:
is this a planet or some orbiting rock?
I see you're black folks here, wherever it is:
is this the Congo? Are you Congolese?
A mask; a masquerade on the Bridge of Sighs!

DE GUICHE

A lady waits for me; so let me past.

CYRANO

A lady? I'm back in Paris at long last!
I've just come down in a thick cosmic shower:
excuse me, various atoms still adhere.
My eyes are full of stardust and comet hairs;
some particles are still stuck to my spurs.

DE GUICHE

Now look . . .

CYRANO

                  I had a fight with the Great Bear
and Neptune plunged his trident up my rear;
fired from Uranus like a shooting star,
my name will live on in the skies up there.
But I aim to put it all in a new book,
and each star sticking to my smoky cloak,
picked up with so much danger, so much risk,
will serve in the printed text as an asterisk —
a work of science, *Empires of the Moon*.

All being well I'll have it finished soon
if I can only keep my nose to the grindstone.

DE GUICHE

Christ, will you let me past, you tedious bore?

CYRANO

(*drawing* DE GUICHE *from the house*)
The seas, the craters . . . Don't you want to hear
about its dark side, the strange creatures there?
You wish to know the means of my ascension?
I used a method of my own invention.
Ignoring fatuous precedent, I've identified
six ways to penetrate the azure bride
and boldly go where none have gone before.
I strip off, bollock naked don't you know . . .

DE GUICHE

Oh, for God's sake.

CYRANO

. . . gleaming from head to toe,
and fasten specimen bottles to arm and thigh
filled with the tear-drops of the morning sky;
the rising sun, sniffing the fragrant dew,
sucks up the bottles and the body too.
. . . A prism of burning mirrors. I ignite
my personal geodesic glitter-crate . . .

DE GUICHE

Your what?

CYRANO

. . . the air gets warm; next thing you know
the heater blows its top and off I go.
. . . Not merely a theorist but a deft technician,
I bounce off into the star-grazing night ocean
on a huge metal insect charged with dynamite,
its intricate spidery structure sprung for flight.

... You must have noticed how smoke rises up?
I fill a globe with smoke and off I pop.

DE GUICHE

But surely . . .

CYRANO

     . . . Here I stand on an iron plate
and throw a magnet at the starry night;
the iron leaps after it; I throw once more
and keep on throwing till I disappear . . .

DE GUICHE

But . . .

CYRANO

     . . . Ebb-tide, the waves drawn up by the moon,
I took a swim, stood out on a sand dune
with salt sea-water clinging to my hair
and rose like an angel through the evening air.
Straight up, along the primrose path, I flew;
and dropped to earth just half an hour ago.
Now the half-hour is over you're free to go:
a marriage has taken place.

DE GUICHE

     What marriage? . . . You,
the voice, the nose: can you be Bergerac?

CYRANO

They exchanged vows just a few minutes back.

Re-enter MUSICIANS, ROXANE, CHRISTIAN, CAPUCHIN,
RAGUENEAU.

DE GUICHE

My compliments, madam; that was a clever notion —
and to you too, inventor and technician:
the detail in your description of the skies

would stop a saint at the gates of paradise.
You should certainly finish that book you spoke about.

CYRANO

I'll send you a signed copy when it comes out.

CAPUCHIN
(*to* DE GUICHE)
A fine couple you've brought together in this house.

DE GUICHE
Yes; take your leave, madame, of your new spouse.
(*to* CHRISTIAN)
. . . The regiment is mustering in full force;
report immediately.

ROXANE
To the front?

DE GUICHE
Of course.

ROXANE

But the cadets aren't going.

DE GUICHE
Oh yes they are.

Hands written order to CHRISTIAN.

Deliver this order to your superiors, sir;
your nuptial night will not be happening yet.

CYRANO
(*aside*)
Something that I, at least, do not regret.

CHRISTIAN
(*to* ROXANE)
Give me another kiss before I go.
(*to* CYRANO)
. . . So difficult to say goodbye.

CYRANO
I know.

DE GUICHE
Enough of this; come on, we're leaving now.

ROXANE
Oh, Cyrano, please look after him for me;
don't let him place his life in jeopardy.

CYRANO
I'll do what I can.

ROXANE
Promise me he'll be careful.

CYRANO
I'll try; but, you know, a soldier's life is awful.

ROXANE
He's to keep warm in those appalling trenches
and not be led astray by country wenches.
Keep him safe; promise he'll take good care
and write often.

CYRANO
Of *that* you can be sure.

Interval

ACT TWO

Marne mud; trenches. Dawn; desolation. DEBRAY, JALOUX; CADETS *asleep in their capes.*

DEBRAY

The fragrant odour of the river Marne.

JALOUX

Marne mud.

DEBRAY

Desolation.

JALOUX

It's nearly dawn.

DEBRAY

A far cry from Paris.

JALOUX

A far cry from Dordogne.

Distant gunfire.

DEBRAY

Damn it!

JALOUX

Swear quietly; keep your voice down.

DEBRAY

The cold; the hunger.

JALOUX

When they dream they dine.

DEBRAY

When you can't get to sleep . . .

Gunfire closer.

CADETS

- Christ, not again!

JALOUX

Could they not give it a rest? Lie down; dream on.

SENTRY
(*off*)

Who's there?

CYRANO
(*off*)

De Bergerac.

SENTRY
(*off*)
Who did you say?

CYRANO
(*off*)

Bergerac, moron.

Enter CYRANO.

DEBRAY
Cyrano, you okay?

CYRANO
(*whispers, shushing* DEBRAY)
They miss on purpose; it's a game we play.

DEBRAY
(*whispers*)
You're mad to risk your life like this each night
to post a letter . . .

CYRANO
I promised he would write.
If she only knew; this boy, so nearly dead
with cold and hunger . . . Still, what a handsome head.

DEBRAY
Go get some sleep yourself.

CYRANO
Don't scold, Debray.
When I slip through the enemy lines I pass a lane
where they lie in a drunken stupor every night.

DEBRAY
Why don't you pick up some provisions, then?

CYRANO
I move fast to get back before first light;
but something's up. If it means what I think it means
we'll all either die today or be full of beans:
I can't be sure.

JALOUX
What a humiliation:
besiegers besieged themselves by malnutrition.

CYRANO
We're certainly at an amusing disadvantage,
besieged by an enemy we ourselves besiege:
perhaps someone will besiege them again out there.

95

DEBRAY

It isn't funny.

CYRANO

It's been known to occur.

DEBRAY

And you risk a life as valuable as your own
to post . . . where now?

CYRANO

To write another one.

Distant gunfire; voices; bugles. CADETS *begin to wake.*

JALOUX

Delicious sleep, goodbye; I know already
exactly what their waking words will be.

BILL

I'm freezing.

JULES

Starving.

JALOUX

Up!

HUGH

Oh, not again.

PATRICK
(*uses sword as a mirror*)
This weather isn't good for the inner man.

BRIAN

I'd give my knighthood for a slice of bread.

JALOUX

Cyrano, this lot are as good as dead
if you don't get over here and help me now
by cheering them up as only you know how.

HUGH

What's that you've got? Is that a wing of grouse?

JULES
(*chewing*)
A bit of tow-rope drizzled with axle-grease:
these parts are not exactly rich in game.

Enter JACQUES *and* GUS *with rod and gun; all crowd round.*

BILL

Look at these sportsmen; where have you two come from?

GUS

A bulging forest.

JACQUES
A salmon-crowded stream.

HUGH

You bagged a pheasant? Got us a few trout?

JACQUES

A shoe.

GUS

A shadow.

JALOUX
Cyrano, help me out!

BILL

We've got to eat; is there nothing to be had?

What's that you're devouring?

CYRANO

Homer's *Iliad*:
not merely nourishment but a mental feast.

JULES

Richelieu, in Paris, guzzles fit to burst.

CYRANO

His greasy eminence might part with a partridge?

BRIAN

Always the witty word, even under siege.

CYRANO

Yes, always the witty word, the well-chosen phrase
spoken in a good cause. When I come to die
give me a rain-washed evening, a clear sky
and the one worthy enemy I recognize,
struck down by the only noble blow there is
on a field of glory far from feverish pillow-slips
with a sword in my hand and a fine phrase on my lips.

Cannon fire; the CADETS *start losing control.*

HUGH

I'm going crazy listening to the thump
of cannon in this pestilential dump.

GUS

I've enteritis, flu, some kind of gripe.

JACQUES

I'm going to shoot myself.

CYRANO

Oh get a grip!

BRIAN

I'll kill you, Cyrano, and boil your nose,
your arse, your ears, your shoulders and your toes;
you probably stuff yourself with cheese and fruit
while you're out roaming the countryside at night.

CYRANO

I make allowances; but be careful, please.

JALOUX

I won't permit disturbances like these.

BRIAN

The Bretons in the next sector refuse to fight
on empty stomachs, and by God they're right.
They say they go 'like spring lambs to the slaughter':
how can they shape up without food and water?
No wonder there's been talk of mutiny;
I've never known such futile ignominy.

JULES

My God I've had it with this fucking war.

JALOUX

You're going to bits; remember who you are!

PATRICK

We're hungry!

CYRANO

Hunger, is that all you can think about?
Bertrand, you were a goat-herd, were you not,
and keep a reed-pipe somewhere in your tights?
Play for this bunch of epicures and sybarites
one of our country airs, gentle and low,
each phrase like a young girl we used to know,
like the local tongue, the cadence of loved voices,
smoke rising from the thatch of farmhouses.

BERTRAND *plays a country air from Languedoc.*

. . . Let your flute, a famished soldier in this place,
recall a time when on its gentle face
your fingers danced a bird-dance, bird to bird;
when, hard-wood now, it once was a soft reed;
let its own song amaze it, so it hears
the wild soul of its own peaceful early years.
. . . Gascons, listen: in his deft hands it's not
a regimental fife but a simple flute;
it's not a shrieking war-whistle the pipe yields
but the sweet wood-wind of our native fields.
Do you see streams, heather, a forest track,
an ancient shepherd in his woven smock,
the rustling river-leaves of the Garonne?
Just listen; we're back in Gascony once again.

JALOUX

They're crying!

CYRANO

Yes, from a hunger of the heart,
a nobler ailment than a grumbling gut.
A visceral substitution shifts the pain;
they forget the misery of the abdomen.

JALOUX

You're going to weaken them with these dreams of home.

CYRANO

No, all we need is a rattling kettle-drum.

Signals to drummer, who briefly rattles his drum.

CADETS
(*springing up*)

What is it? Action? Have the enemy come?

CYRANO

. . . You see? Goodbye nostalgia, woods and hills;
what the reed-pipe evokes the drum dispels.

Enter DE GUICHE.

BRIAN

De Guiche.

CYRANO

No friend of yours?

BRIAN

A pain in the arse,
him and his shining armour trimmed with lace,
iron hand and velvet glove. I expect he's here
with us country squires to play the grand seigneur.

JALOUX

A Gascon, though.

BILL

Not like the rest of us;
a Gascon should be wired up to the moon —
nothing more dangerous than a rational one.

GUS

He's pale.

JACQUES

He's ravenous, just like everyone,
even with a midriff glittering in the sun.

CYRANO

Don't let him think we're suffering; you lot start
a game of poker, while I read Descartes.

DE GUICHE

(*to* JALOUX)

Good morning; you look haggard round the eyes.

JALOUX

(*to* DE GUICHE)

You look as if you haven't slept for days.

DE GUICHE

(*surveys* CADETS)

So these are the malcontents, the mutinous clique
who've made me into an object of dislike.
I hear on all sides that you mountainy squires,
you sons of Gascony and the remoter shires,
malign your colonel wherever you see fit
as a cold schemer, prominent at court,
because I wear kid gloves and a clean shirt.
It's my belief what really gets your goat,
you rough nobility, is the unusual thought
that one might be a Gascon through and through
without being a provincial ruffian too;
but I won't ask your captain to punish you.

JALOUX

In any case the question doesn't arise;
they're my recruits, I pay their salaries
and only obey war orders.

DE GUICHE

That may be so;
anyhow I can face down this bravado.
My conduct under fire has been widely hailed,
like yesterday's action in the upper field.

CYRANO

And your white scarf?

DE GUICHE
(*pleased*)
You heard about that?

CYRANO

Indeed.

DE GUICHE
(*shiftily*)
To my surprise, while rallying my men,
I found myself too close to the enemy line,
shoved there by a crowd of fugitives; instead,
mildly alarmed, I had the imagination
to drop my white scarf of identification.
I might be a prisoner now, or among the dead,
had I not thrown off that sign of privilege,
regrouped my force and led a further charge.
What do you think?

CYRANO
Just this: the great Henri Quatre,
even faced with multitudes and shown no quarter,
would never have sacrificed, however rash,
the distinctive emblem of his white panache.

The CADETS *listen with quiet pleasure.*

DE GUICHE
It worked, though.

CYRANO
Certainly; but one doesn't shirk
the honour of bearing a distinguishing mark.
Our views of courage differ in this, at least:
if I'd been present when the scarf was lost
I'd have picked it up and worn it myself. Let's swop
and I'll wear it this morning if we go over the top.

DE GUICHE

You know quite well it's sunk in the mud somewhere,
in a field churned up long since by cannon fire.
It would be pointless looking for it out there.

CYRANO

Too risky too; however, I have it here.

DE GUICHE

. . . Thank you; with this cloth I can semaphore
a signal I was reluctant to send before . . .

He waves the scarf from a parapet.

You see?

SENTRY
(*off*)
Stop, who goes there?

Gunfire.

DE GUICHE

                    That noise you hear
is a double agent, working for our side.
He gives them pseudo-facts that I provide;
directing them with our disinformation,
we have control of the larger situation.

CYRANO

A lousy spy.

DE GUICHE

         Yes, but a useful one.
While you were snoring, two hours before dawn,
the staff, in a brave bid to re-provision,
set off in silence for our rear position
with guard units; ours is a tricky case
since half the army have returned to base.

JALOUX

Our plight is desperate but not serious, though,
if the enemy don't know.

DE GUICHE

Ah, but they do;
there's going to be a final push; my spy
was here to warn me it will come today.
'I can't,' said he, 'be certain exactly where:
which point in your defences would you prefer?
I'll tell them that's the vulnerable side
and that's where they'll attack'; so I replied:
'I get you; keep a close watch on our line
and go for the point at which you see my sign.'

JALOUX

Gentlemen, let's get ready; we've one hour.

BILL

Let's finish our card-game; we've an hour to spare.

DE GUICHE

We must buy time; the staff will be back soon.

JALOUX

And to buy time?

DE GUICHE

Why, between now and noon
lay down your lives, if you would be so kind.

CYRANO

So this is the vengeance that you have in mind?

DE GUICHE

I won't pretend that, had I liked you more,
I'd still have picked you for this tedious chore;
but, since you're famous for your cutting edge,
I serve the king in serving my own rage.

I know you like to engage with a hundred men;
there'll be a thousand now, so you can't complain.

Exit DE GUICHE.

CYRANO
Now, lads, to the Gascon arms of gold and blue
we're adding some arterial crimson too.
. . . Christian?

CHRISTIAN
Roxane.

CYRANO
I know.

CHRISTIAN
I need to send
a last, heartfelt letter before . . . the end.

CYRANO
I thought that might be needed; I have it here.

CHRISTIAN
Show me, I have to read it.

CYRANO
Are you quite sure?

CYRANO *shows the letter.*

CHRISTIAN
Of course . . . Good heavens.

CYRANO
What?

CHRISTIAN
This funny smear:

that's not a blot or a rain-drop; that's a tear.

CYRANO
A poet dedicates himself to his exercise.
So poignant, this last letter, to my surprise
I felt real tears spring into my own eyes.

CHRISTIAN
Real tears?

CYRANO
Yes, death itself is not so bad;
but not to see her again, that's what's so sad —
to think that I . . . that neither of us will ever . . .

CHRISTIAN
Give me the letter.

CYRANO *hands it over; a rumble of wheels.*

SENTRY
(*off*)
Stop right there, whoever
you are!

·JALOUX
What's this, more spies?

SENTRY
(*off*)
It's a coach, sir.

Enter ROXANE *in a coach; two coachmen.*

JALOUX
A private coach?

CHRISTIAN
(*to* ROXANE)
Roxane, are you insane?

ROXANE
It's gone on far too long, this dull campaign.

CYRANO
(*aside*)
God, dare I look at her?

Re-enter DE GUICHE.

DE GUICHE
(*to* ROXANE)
You can't stay here.

ROXANE
Of course I can; have you a drum to spare?

A CADET *provides a drum; she sits.*

CYRANO
How did you find us?

ROXANE
                          Simply followed the signs —
you mean, how did I get through the enemy lines?
A ruined countryside, a sort of hell;
but, like the pumpkin in the fairy tale,
we just drove furiously, as if by magic
and under cover of a moonless night
through devastation little short of tragic:
if this is war I don't think much of it.
(*proudly*) We were stopped briefly by a night patrol!
I stuck my head out and, with a friendly smile,
explained that I was going to meet my lover;
they clicked their heels and the incident was over.
'My husband' is what I should have said, I know;

but if I had, they'd never have let me through.

DE GUICHE

There's going to be blue murder within the hour.

CYRANO

Colonel de Guiche has made that certain sure.

ROXANE
(*to* DE GUICHE)

Do you want to make me a widow?

DE GUICHE

Upon my word . . .

ROXANE

I'm going to see some action, I've decided;
besides, I've never been to a war before.

CYRANO

Our *précieuse* is a heroine, is that it?

ROXANE

Cyrano, I'm your cousin, don't forget.

PATRICK

We'll take good care of you.

ROXANE

And I of you.

JACQUES

Strange, there's a scent of violets in the dew.

CYRANO

This looks like a quiet sector, standing here,
but once the fighting starts you've no idea . . .

ROXANE

Oh yes, I know, the frightfulness of war,
the shock and awe, the heroism, the gore,
and horrors such as I've never seen before,
gratuitous, unimaginable, inhuman —
you know about these things; I'm just a woman,
naïve and inexperienced, but who
says that a woman can't be a soldier too?
I've equipped myself with a special cap and pin;
if the colonel leaves perhaps we can begin.

DE GUICHE

I have to inspect what cannon we have to hand
and that should give you time to change your mind.

Exit.

CADETS

She's staying; so let's clean up. A comb; a brush;
a razor! A pair of clippers for my moustache!

CYRANO

I'm asking you for the last time to think twice.

ROXANE

Nonsense; nothing would make me leave this place.

JALOUX

Perhaps, in the circumstances, I might introduce
some of these unreformed reactionaries
who will have the honour of dying before your eyes?
. . . Lord Bill Cro-Magnon de Lascaux du Zou;
Jules-Jeroboam des Caveaux de Castignac;
Patrick de Château-Lynch; Lord Mont-Aigu;
Sir Brian de Castel-Trembletower; Sir Hugh
Dulac des Cariboux; Gus Meaulnes; Sir Jacques
Chirac; Lord Obélisque de l'Estomac.

ROXANE

You're all knights and barons?

PATRICK

Most of us are.

JALOUX

Madame, please drop your handkerchief.

ROXANE

What for?

JALOUX

We need a pennant to keep our line in place.

ROXANE
(*drops her handkerchief*)

It's rather modest.

JALOUX
(*ties it to a lance*)
Yes, but it's made of lace.

GUS

Having seen this angel I would gladly croak
if only I'd a hazel-nut to crack.

JALOUX

To speak of food when such an exquisite . . .

ROXANE

But it's nippy here; I too could use a bite —
a drumstick and a sip of wine, all right?

JACQUES

Where would we find such things?

ROXANE *points to coach.*

ROXANE

Why, over there,
tucked up beneath the back seat of the car.
My driver, whom I think you already know,
looks after the provisions.

RAGUENEAU *appears from coach with provisions.*

CADETS

It's Ragueneau!

CYRANO

(*to* ROXANE)

Good fairy.

RAGUENEAU

Gentlemen!

CADET

Bravo; bravo . . . !

RAGUENEAU *and* COACHMEN *distribute provisions.*

RAGUENEAU

This fine piece being clearly to their *taste,*
the enemy let us past with our *repast;*
so *game* they never noticed the *game pie;*
so heart-stricken, so keen on *venery,*
they missed the *venison;* so quick to bare
their heads, they never glimpsed the camem-*bert;*
so blind with beauty and in so much pain
they overlooked these magnums of cham-*pagne!*

GUS

Look, truffled peacock! We won't die, at least,
without a proper blast . . . I mean a feast.

The CADETS *eat ravenously.*

CYRANO
(*to* ROXANE)
I need to speak to you before you two talk.

ROXANE
(*to* CADETS)
All for you lads, even if de Guiche comes back.
You've lots of time; don't eat at such a rate.
Knives and forks; and, captain, where's *your* plate?
Christian, make yourself useful . . . Red or white?

CHRISTIAN
Nothing for me.

ROXANE
Come on, you have to eat.

CHRISTIAN
Oh, why on earth did you come here in the first place?

ROXANE
It was my duty; now, put on a brave face.

Enter DE GUICHE.

CYRANO
Quick, hide this stuff. Adopt a nonchalant air
as if nothing's happened. Ragueneau, back in the car.

RAGUENEAU *and* COACHMEN *hide in the coach.*

DE GUICHE
Why are you all so red in the face?

BILL
War fever.

DE GUICHE
You're looking very pleased with yourselves; however

you'll have one cannon only, behind the ridge,
to use as you see fit when the enemy charge.
It's a new kind, so watch out for the recoil.

                    JULES
We don't re-(*hic*)-coil.

                         DE GUICHE
                    You're stocious!

                         JULES
                                        On motor-oil.

                         BRIAN
D'you hear that? — 'Stocious', in the Gascon style.

                         DE GUICHE
Madame, have you decided to stay or go?

                         ROXANE
I'm staying.

                         DE GUICHE
                    In that case I shall be staying too.

                         CYRANO
At last, monsieur, a truly noble gesture.

                         HUGH
He's a real Gascon under the vest-(*hic*)-iture.

                         DE GUICHE
I don't desert a lady when she's in danger.

                         BILL
Let's give the bugger something for his hunger.

                         DE GUICHE
Do you think I'd pick at your left-over stuff?

CYRANO
Well said.

PATRICK
I believe he's a Gascon sure enough.

JALOUX
(*to* ROXANE)
My front line are in place; shall we take a look?

Exit ROXANE *and* JALOUX.

CHRISTIAN
What's the big secret?

CYRANO
About Roxane . . .

CHRISTIAN
Be quick.

CYRANO
You wrote to her more often than you know;
I didn't tell you.

CHRISTIAN
How did you get through?

CYRANO
I'd slip, under cover of darkness, behind their lines.

CHRISTIAN
How often have I written? Three times, four times?

CYRANO
Twice daily.

CHRISTIAN
You're so caught up in this adventure

you risked death for it?

CYRANO
Shhh, not where she can hear.

Re-enter ROXANE *and* JALOUX.

ROXANE
Now, Christian.

CHRISTIAN
Now, Roxane, please tell me why
you thought it necessary to come here today.
You negotiate dangerous roads and muddy ditches;
you might have been raped or killed.

ROXANE
Your sweet dispatches
drove me mad with desire; just try to recall
how often you've written to me in the past while.

CHRISTIAN
A few love letters . . .

ROXANE
You can't know; be quiet.
I've loved you ever since that midsummer night
beneath my window where, in a new tone,
you opened your ardent heart to me alone.
Reading your letters I seemed to hear again
the tender night-voice that entranced me then.
I read and re-read, until my own heart was full,
those pages, each a leaf blown from your soul,
each redolent of a love potent and sincere.

CHRISTIAN
Sincere; potent? . . . And that's what brings you here?

I've come to apologize for being so frivolous
as to have fallen for you, before all this,
solely because of your fine physical grace:
what better moment than if death is near?
Now, like a bird that hops before it flies,
it's the true spirit in you I recognize;
you've triumphed over your beauty, I see you whole
and now I adore you only for your soul.
Be glad; since to be loved for the outward show
must be a torment to a man like you;
for me your soaring thoughts obscure your face,
and the features that so pleased me in the first place,
seeing clearly, I no longer see.

CHRISTIAN
I see.

ROXANE
I can see you don't believe in this love one bit.

CHRISTIAN
Roxane, these soaring thoughts you talk about,
this soul stuff, I want nothing to do with it;
I'd rather you loved me as I used to be.

ROXANE
The way the girls would love you in the past?
Be loved now in a superior way at last.

CHRISTIAN
It was better before.

ROXANE
No, this is more profound;
if you were ugly . . .

CHRISTIAN
No!

117

ROXANE

. . . you might understand.

CHRISTIAN

If I were ugly?

ROXANE

I would love you best.

CHRISTIAN

My God, did you say *ugly*? Do you mean
if I'd a disfigurement like some other men
you'd love me with a new kind of devotion
greater than merely physical admiration?
Do you want somebody with enormous ears,
one eye, or an exaggerated nose?
Would you really prefer ugliness in a man?

ROXANE

We've had too much of beauty, too many dreams;
the world is even more beautiful than it seems
if we can penetrate the outward show
and rescue the true spirit hidden below.
Do you understand me? Are you happier now?

CHRISTIAN
(*glumly*)

Of course.

ROXANE

What's wrong?

CHRISTIAN

I need some time alone.
Roxane, go give those gallant chaps a smile;
they're all going to die in a little while.

ROXANE *squeezes his hand and goes to* CADETS, CHRISTIAN *to*
CYRANO.

... Cyrano?

CYRANO
What's the matter, you look pale.

CHRISTIAN
She doesn't love me; she loves you, you fool.
She only loves my soul, and that means you;
you love her too.

CYRANO
No, no.

CHRISTIAN
Oh yes you do;
madly, admit it.

CYRANO
... Yes, I'm afraid it's true.

CHRISTIAN
So tell her.

CYRANO
No.

CHRISTIAN
Why not?

CYRANO
Look at my snout.

CHRISTIAN
She'd love me, even ugly.

CYRANO
She said that?
The fact she even thought it pleases me,
but don't take any of this too literally.

Don't *you* start getting ugly, or madame
will want me even uglier than I am.

CHRISTIAN
So tell her everything, let her make her choice.

CYRANO
No, that's a torture I could never face.

CHRISTIAN
It's not fair; I can't steal your happiness.

CYRANO
Should I steal yours because I have a knack
for high-flown rhetoric and ingenious talk,
a natural aptitude for poetic drivel?

CHRISTIAN
I'm fed up being my own greatest rival.
Our marriage vows, clandestine as they were,
can be annulled if we ever get out of here:
I want to be loved for myself, not my appearance.
I'm going to see what's happening down there
but I'll be back; speak to her; ask her preference.

CYRANO
It will be you.

CHRISTIAN
Perhaps . . . Roxane?

CYRANO
Oh, no . . .

CHRISTIAN
(*to* ROXANE)
Your cousin has something important to say to you.

ROXANE

Important?

CHRISTIAN
Yes, important for you and him;
I'm just going down to the lines and may be some time.

Exit.

ROXANE
A darling, yes, but such a puzzling youth.

CYRANO
Are you quite sure you told him the whole truth?

Gunfire.

ROXANE
I said I'd love him even if he . . .

CYRANO
Go ahead —
even if he were ugly, I think you said;
even deformed?

ROXANE
Deformed.

CYRANO
Grotesque?

ROXANE
Grotesque,
I'd love him even more; why do you ask?

CYRANO
My God, perhaps it's true. Listen, Roxane . . .

He takes her hand; CADETS *bring in* CHRISTIAN, *dying, and form a group around him.*

DEBRAY
(*quietly*)

Cyrano!

CYRANO

What? . . . I see.

He drops her hand.

ROXANE

Has the war begun?

CYRANO
(*aside*)

I can never speak to her about this again.

ROXANE

What's going on there?

CYRANO

Nothing.

ROXANE

But those men . . .
what did you want to say to me earlier on?

CYRANO

Christian had, *has* the soul of a fine young man.

ROXANE

Had the soul . . . ? Christian? Christian!

CYRANO

He's nearly gone;
he took the first shot from an enemy gun.

She kneels beside CHRISTIAN.

JALOUX
Eyes on the wood; wait for the word!

CHRISTIAN
. . . Roxane . . .

CYRANO
I told her everything and she chooses you.

CHRISTIAN *dies.*

ROXANE
He's getting cold; this letter, for me too?

CYRANO
(aside)
. . . My letter! . . .

JALOUX
Fire!

CADETS *fire.*

CYRANO
Roxane, I have to go.

ROXANE
He's dead; stay with me for a minute or so.
Wasn't he a great spirit, a noble creature,
a sublime poet and a generous nature?
He's dead . . .

CYRANO
(aside)
And so am I now; her tears flow
for both of us, though she must never know.

ROXANE

Blood and tears on the letter . . .

VOICE

(*off*)

Surrender now!

CADETS *fire*.

DE GUICHE

Hang on, our reinforcements are at the bridge!

CYRANO

Get her away from here; we're going to charge.

RAGUENEAU

God in heaven! . . . She's fainted.

DE GUICHE

Over the top!

VOICE

(*off*)

Disarm and show yourselves; we're coming up!

CYRANO

You've proved your valour, sir; now get her clear.

DE GUICHE

We'll win yet if your men can hold them here.

CYRANO

We'll keep them occupied. Roxane, goodbye.

JALOUX

We're weakening; I've been wounded in the thigh.

CYRANO

Trust me; I've two deaths to avenge, old friend:

124

Christian's, and that of my own peace of mind.
Hearten us now, you innocent lace handkerchief.
Get down there; head them off; Bertrand, the fife!

BERTRAND *plays a war cry.*

CADETS

They're coming up.

CYRANO

We fight to the last breath.

Intense fire; CADETS *fall.*

VOICE
(*off*)

Who are these madmen so in love with death?

CYRANO
(*shouts*)

These are the Gascon Cadets
Of Captain de Castel-Jaloux:
Christ, what a bunch of shits,
What an unspeakable crew . . . Charge!

He charges with the few surviving CADETS; BERTRAND'S *war
cry; cannon smoke.*

A convent garden; autumn evening. SISTERS MARGUERITE, ANNE,
CLAIRE *etc.* ROXANE, *in black, sits at an easel, brush in hand.*

ANNE

This morning after matins Sister Claire
admired her new coif in a hand mirror.

I can't think why; it's not so very smart.

CLAIRE

Sister Anne stole a prune from a prune tart
in the refectory; I saw her, I was there.

MARGUERITE

I shall report you both to monsieur Cyrano
when he arrives this evening.

NUNS

Oh no, no!

CLAIRE

He'll say we eat too much.

ANNE

He'll think we're vain;
he'll tease us about being nuns again.

CLAIRE

Reverend Mother, is it true he's come
each Saturday for months at the same time?

MARGUERITE

As long as his widowed cousin wants to remain
here in the convent silence where she grieves,
she says, like a raven mourning among doves;
only he can distract her from her pain.

CLAIRE

He's so funny, with such a kindly touch:
no wonder we like Saturdays so much!

ANNE

I think he's a bit of an atheist even so.

CLAIRE

Well, let's convert him back.

MARGUERITE

Convert him? No,
don't even think of it; don't plague the man
or he may come less often than hitherto.
God knows all about monsieur Cyrano.

ANNE

Each Saturday, full of mischief, he lets drop:
'Last night, Friday, I murdered a lamb chop.'

MARGUERITE

Sometimes he eats nothing from day to day:
he's poor, you know.

ANNE

Who told you?

MARGUERITE

Monsieur Debray.
At an age when most men think of settling down
he's still living in two cheap rooms in town.

ANNE

Doesn't anyone help him?

MARGUERITE

No, he's far too proud —
but look, a visitor; let's go inside.

Enter DE GUICHE, *now Duke de Gramont.*

ANNE

The Duke de Gramont.

CLAIRE
(*wistfully*)
Yes, in the latest fashions.

ANNE
He seldom comes now.

CLAIRE
Worldly preoccupations.

Exit NUNS *to house.*

DE GUICHE
You intend to live here, lovely to no purpose,
always in mourning?

ROXANE
Yes.

DE GUICHE
Still faithful?

ROXANE
Yes.

DE GUICHE
Have you forgiven me?

ROXANE
We are here to forgive.

DE GUICHE
Was he really . . . ?

ROXANE
A great boy; so fine, so brave.

DE GUICHE
I never really knew him, I must admit.

His last letter: still next to your heart?

ROXANE

I keep it on this pendant round my neck,
folded in velvet, as a last relique.

DE GUICHE

You love him even in death?

ROXANE

I think sometimes
he's still alive; he speaks to me in dreams.
His love drifts in the scent of mint and thyme.

DE GUICHE

Cyrano comes to see you from time to time?

ROXANE

Regularly; an old friend now, he sits
under this tree and tells me his 'gazettes',
the weekly news, while I paint some leafy scene.
I know his step, I don't even have to turn —
the clock strikes six; at the last stroke his cane
comes tapping down the steps and up the lane.
They bring this armchair out if the weather's fine.
He makes fun of my amateurish art,
chuckling at my pictorial aspiration,
provides me with the latest information
and itemizes the goings-on at court.

Enter DEBRAY.

DE GUICHE

How is our friend?

DEBRAY

Not good.

ROXANE

Oh, don't mind him.

DEBRAY

Everything I predicted: poverty, solitude, ostracism.
He makes new enemies daily with his sarcasm,
mocking social pretension, conventional cant,
new fashions, phonies, even the government.

ROXANE

Cyrano knows how to protect himself.

DEBRAY

That's not what troubles me; it's the empty shelf,
the cold fog of winter, the icy rain
in his bare attic through the broken pane:
those are the killers who will do him in.
His waist shrinks daily by a centimetre,
his nose has grown the colour of old pewter;
he's nothing to keep him warm but a frayed coat.

DE GUICHE

He's no rich parvenu in a shiny suit.
Don't feel too sorry for him even so;
he came to his own decision long ago
to be a free man both in deed and thought.
He's poor, I've everything; I understand —
still, I'd be more than proud to shake his hand.
I'll leave you now . . . Goodbye.

ROXANE

I'll see you out.

DE GUICHE

Sometimes I envy your amazing cousin —
when life's rewards have been too easily won,
through no particular wickedness of one's own,
one feels recurrent twinges of self-disgust
which add up, not to remorse, but a vague unrest.

130

While one ascends the glittering steps of power
the ducal robe trails in its dusty fur,
as the leaves whisper in your trailing skirts,
a rustle of lost illusions and vain regrets.

ROXANE

You're very philosophical.

DE GUICHE

Yes . . . Monsieur,
it's true what the lady says, nobody dare
challenge our friend, but he's made many foes.
I had it yesterday from one who knows:
he's to be very careful when he goes out,
his personal safety may be under threat;
he should lie low . . .

DEBRAY

What, Cyrano lie low?
He's due today; I'll warn him, but you know . . .

Enter ANNE *and* RAGUENEAU.

ANNE

Madame, another visitor: monsieur Ragueneau.

Exit ANNE.

ROXANE
(*to* DEBRAY)

A failed poet, actor and tabloid hack,
he comes to me with tales of infinite woe.
(*to* RAGUENEAU)
. . . Tell monsieur Debray your troubles; I'll be back.

Exit ROXANE *with* DE GUICHE.

RAGUENEAU

It's best she doesn't hear . . . Our friend de Bergerac . . .

going to call on him, I saw some bloke
against the skyline on a new building site
drop a breeze-block on him: a direct hit.
It didn't *look* deliberate, but it struck
Cyrano on the skull with a mighty crack.
Running across there, quick as I could, I found
him stretched out in the mud with a head wound.

DEBRAY

He's dead?

RAGUENEAU

Not dead; I took him up to his flat,
his living quarters if you can call them that,
his studio, his observatory . . .

DEBRAY

He's in pain?

RAGUENEAU

Not in pain, no, unconscious; the doctor said
something about an injury to the brain.
He's lying there with bandages round his head:
let's go, there's no one else beside his bed.
He'll probably die if he tries to stand up straight.

DEBRAY

Come through the chapel; it's the quickest route.

Exit DEBRAY *and* RAGUENEAU; *re-enter* ROXANE, *who resumes
her work.*

ROXANE

Give me the silence of this autumn park
where grief relaxes, not the violent shock
of stormy April with its weeping fits;
and the great chair where cousin Cyrano sits.

The chapel bell rings a quick six o'clock angelus.

Six o'clock; so why is he not here yet?
Amazing if, for the first time, he were late.
. . . Dead leaves, dead lives . . . Aha, I hear his stick.
Good evening to you, monsieur de Bergerac;
this purple, I can't seem to make it work.
You're late for the first time.

Enter ANNE *and* CYRANO, *his head bandaged beneath his hat,*
ANNE *shocked by his appearance.* ROXANE *goes on with her work.*

CYRANO
But here at last —
delayed, I'm afraid, by an unexpected guest.

ROXANE
Someone annoying?

CYRANO
Maddening; so I say,
'Excuse me, please, today is Saturday,
a day when I have a regular rendezvous
with an old friend; come back in an hour or two' —
though I may have to leave you before then.

ROXANE
You won't tease Sister Anne?

CYRANO
Ah, Sister Anne,
you with your fine eyes permanently cast down.
. . . Shh, not a word. I ate a whole cow last night.

ANNE
Did you indeed? So that's why you look so white . . .
afterwards, promise, I want you to come up
to the refectory for a nice hot bowl of soup.

ROXANE
Is she converting you?

CYRANO
No fear of that,
she's given up trying; but I tell you what:
this evening, Sister, pause in the chapel nave
and pray for my poor soul.

ANNE
I already have.

Exit ANNE; CYRANO *sits.*

CYRANO
I see you're still at the old leafy pictures.

ROXANE
I've been expecting your harsh critical strictures.
. . . The leaves are dying.

CYRANO
Yes, with a gentle crash
as if to demonstrate a last panache
in the fall from air to earth, from earth to ash;
as if, despite the fear of eternal night,
they wished their death to have the grace of flight.

ROXANE
You're melancholy this evening?

CYRANO
No I'm not.

ROXANE
Let's leave the leaves; I'm waiting for my 'gazette'.

CYRANO
(*clears his throat*)
. . . Sunday last, having eaten too much cake,
the monarch had a high fever and it took
several injections to draw off the poison

and execute the fever for high treason.
Monday, raising the siege, our armies won,
at last, a glorious victory at Verdun.
Tuesday, the royal gala, a thousand candle
were burnt for throwing light on so much scandal.
Wednesday, holed up in a special train,
the enemy signed a ceasefire at Compiègne.
Aurélia's little pekinese still lives
thanks to a vigorous course of laxatives.
Illumineuse has taken a new beau;
Thursday, the whole court was at Fontainebleau.
. . . Friday, *rien*; nothing . . .

ROXANE
Cousin, what's wrong?

CYRANO
Nothing, nothing; my old wound from the Marne.
It's nothing, it soon passes; now it's gone.

ROXANE
Each of us has our wounds; I too have mine —
still there, eating my heart out, the old pain
under a letter yellowing round the ears
where I can still make out the blood and tears.

CYRANO
His letter, yes: didn't you once promise me
you'd let me read it?

ROXANE
I did certainly.
Would you like to read it now?

CYRANO
Yes, if I may.

She hands it over; he reads aloud.

'. . . Roxane, goodbye, I think I'm about to die . . .'

ROXANE

You're going to read it aloud?

CYRANO

'. . . perhaps today.
My soul calls out to you with unspoken cries —
never again to rest my dazzled eyes
on yours, never again to watch your slight
unconscious gestures in their gentle flight:
for instance the head-scratching, yours alone,
the strange hair-fiddling you have made your own . . .'

ROXANE

The way you read . . . I've heard that voice before.

CYRANO *reads from memory; twilight.*

CYRANO

'. . . the only woman I have learnt to adore . . . ;
goodbye, my love . . .'

ROXANE

That voice is one I know.

Unknown to him, she stands behind him, looking over his shoulder.

CYRANO

' . . . Even in the other world to which I go
I who have loved you beyond words, I who . . .'

ROXANE

It's growing dark; how can you read it now?

*Startled, he turns round with a frightened gesture. A long silence;
she takes his hands.*

. . . And meantime, all these months, you've played the part

of the friend who comes to lighten my sad heart.
I should have guessed it when you spoke my name.

CYRANO

No, no; I never . . .

ROXANE

It was you all the time!

I see now through the whole generous device —
really, cousin, what an heroic choice!
The letters, they were yours, each ardent word;
and the night voice, it was *your* voice I heard!

CYRANO

I've never loved you as you think, Roxane.

ROXANE

Oh, yes you do.

CYRANO

No, that was a different man.

ROXANE

You're whispering now, as if you don't believe . . .

CYRANO

No, no, I've never loved you . . . my dearest love.

ROXANE

. . . So much is dead; so much begins to live.
Why have you been so silent? These are your tears
here on the writing-paper . . .

CYRANO

The blood is his.

ROXANE

Why break your sublime silence here tonight?

Re-enter DEBRAY *and* RAGUENEAU.

DEBRAY

I knew he'd come as usual; I was right.
Madame, he shouldn't have risen from his bed.
A crazy gesture: Cyrano, are you mad?

ROXANE

Just now I saw him break out in a sweat.

CYRANO

True, I haven't yet finished my gazette:
Monsieur de Bergerac, on his way from town
an hour ago, was treacherously struck down.

Uncovers his head; ROXANE *rises.*

ROXANE

His head in bandages: what does he mean?
Cyrano, who did this to you and why?

CYRANO

Not, as I once said, 'under a clear sky
and the one worthy enemy I recognize,
struck down by the only noble blow there is';
for fate plays tricks on us and I've taken a knock
from a hired killer with a concrete block.
I've made a hash of my life, and even my death.

RAGUENEAU
(*sobs*)

Monsieur de Bergerac . . . !

CYRANO

Ragueneau, save your breath.
What are you up to now, my old confrère?

RAGUENEAU

I work as a candle-snuffer for Molière.

CYRANO

Molière?

RAGUENEAU

Molière; but I'll be quitting soon.
He opened last night in a new play and I swear
he's stolen a whole scene from a piece of your own —
a whole scene, it has to be seen to be believed.

CYRANO

That doesn't matter: was it well received?

RAGUENEAU

They were in stitches.

CYRANO

Life has been just like that,
being the prompter no one knows about
and shining only with reflected glory.
Roxane . . . the balcony? My life story —
cloaked in the dark, a man whom no one sees,
while someone else ascends the jasmine trees
and claims the wonderful, the ultimate prize;
yet I acknowledge, since I'm dying now,
Molière's genius and Christian's noble brow.

Bell; organ; moonrise.

CYRANO

The bell rings and the angels go to prayer.

ROXANE
(*calls*)

Sister; Sister!

CYRANO

No, don't interfere;
when you come back I probably won't be here.
I lacked only harmony and there we are:

sphere music, the music of a lonely star.

ROXANE

Don't die; I love you.

CYRANO

No, when in the story-books
she tells the prince she loves him, his ill looks
dissolve like darkness in the morning light;
but, as you see, I haven't changed a bit.

ROXANE

It's my fault!

CYRANO

Au contraire; as a boy I never
tasted womanly kindness, since my mother
disliked me, and I had no sister either.
As a young lover I felt scarcely human,
listening always for the sudden laugh;
but now I've known the friendship of a woman.
Thanks to your presence, I can say with relief
some feminine grace has lightened my dark life.

DEBRAY *indicates the moon.*

DEBRAY

Your other friend is here.

CYRANO

I see her, yes.

ROXANE
(*sobs*)
I loved the one man and I've lost him twice!

CYRANO
(*to the moon*)
Bright minerals; a mysterious opal silence:

no tears drop from *that* ambiguous face.
Tonight, without benefit of rocket science,
I could walk on air to my chosen paradise.
Old friends will be there before my naked eyes
— Copernicus, Galileo and Socrates . . .

                    DEBRAY
No, no, it's too outrageous; I protest!
A great spirit, a great heart: what a waste,
to die like this!

                    CYRANO
            Your moaning's getting worse.
. . . These are the Gascon . . . Hubble is right, of course:
the constant increase of the universe,
those infinite spaces . . .

                    DEBRAY
            Delirium now, you hear?

                    CYRANO
Poet, composer, astronaut, philosopher
and a great lover though nobody loved him back,
now here lies Cyrano de Bergerac —
so gifted, with so little to show for it.
Excuse me now, I can no longer wait.
. . . Sea of Darkness, Sea of Tranquility, Sea of Dreams,
you'll find me somewhere in those quiet realms;
I'm going to take off now with the moonbeams . . .
Continue to mourn Christian; I only ask
that when the great cold has begun its task
your grief include me, if there is some to spare.
Nymph, in thine orisons . . . Not here, not here;
I refuse to die at peace in an armchair.
Nobody help, please, nobody interfere;
I only want this tree at my backside . . .

    Rises; goes to tree.

No eyes or nose, he's coming; clothed in lead,
I'll meet him with drawn sword, the cadaverous clown,
my laser blade piercing his empty skull.

Draws sword; fences with shadows.

What is he staring at, does he stare me down?
It's a lost cause, but we don't fight to win.
A thousand of you now, my back to the wall?
Old adversaries, I recognize you all —
prejudice, cowardice, compromise, stupidity.
Make terms with you? No, over my dead body.
You bad bastards have cornered me already
and I've no doubt you've done for me tonight
but even so I fight; I fight; I fight!

He falls, exhausted, against the tree, supported by ROXANE.

. . . Though they've co-opted everything in sight,
the rose and laurel both, all love and art,
something vital survives that they can't wreck —
something I wear, something of mine I take
to heaven tonight; and when I bow before
the threshold, brushing the clouds from the blue door,
it will dance there, a flourish, a white flash
I carry off regardless . . .

ROXANE
(*kisses him*)
What; what?

CYRANO
. . . My panache.